INTERESTING STORIES

FOR

CURIOUS MINDS

A COLLECTION OF MIND-BOGGLING
TRUE STORIES ABOUT HISTORY, SCIENCE,
POP CULTURE AND JUST ABOUT
EVERYTHING IN BETWEEN

BILL O'NEILL

ISBN: 978-1-64845-101-0

Contents

DON'T FORGET YOUR FREE BOOKS

GET THEM AT WWW.TRIVIABILL.COM

Introduction

What do you know about Henry VIII?

Chances are, you know that he had six wives. And you probably also know the rhyme recalling the fate of all those unhappy spouses: *Divorced, Beheaded, Died; Divorced, Beheaded, Survived.*

Perhaps you know too that he was the father of Elizabeth I, Mary I, and his much longed-for son, the short-lived Edward VI. And, depending on how much of a history buff you are, you might also know about his war with the European church - which led to the destruction of many of England's holiest sites (the so-called "Dissolution of the Monasteries"). It also eventually paved the way for the formation of the Church of England, driving his Anglican followers apart from the Catholic Church forever.

But did you also know that when he was 29 years old, the young king challenged his French counterpart, King Francis I of France, to a wrestling match?

This literal battle royale took place in 1520, at a grand meeting of European royalty known to historians as the Field of the Cloth of Gold. The meeting was the result of Henry, Francis, and their Spanish counterpart, Charles V, agreeing to sign a treaty allying their military forces against the ever-growing and increasingly powerful Ottoman Empire in the far east of Europe. That treaty was proposed in 1518; Henry and Francis agreed to meet somewhere neutral as a sign of their friendship in 1519; and in the summer of 1520, the pair finally convened at Calais, a small port and former English-held stronghold on the north coast of France.

The event was so grand that it almost bankrupted the two nations - and when the two rival kings began to literally brawl with one another, it was touch and go whether the uneasy alliance would even last at all. But happily, the two kings took the impromptu wrestling match in good faith.

According to reports, the whole thing was Henry's idea: having always been a robust and powerful man, he felt he had met a good physical match in Francis, who gamely accepted the king's request for a fight. With youth on his side (Francis was six years younger than Henry), the French king allegedly won the fight with ease, yet despite his notoriously fierce temper, Henry took the loss in his stride and the two left the field as firm friends.

In retrospect, you would be forgiven for thinking this tale sounds almost a little too extraordinary to be true. Two of Europe's most significant historical figures, literally rolling around on the ground, battling one another in a test of physical strength, surrounded by the most lavish event the continent had ever seen? It's certainly bizarre—and yet, it is entirely true.

And what's more, so too are all the other INTERESTING STORIES that follow this one...

The Devil's Footprints

The Victorians were notoriously superstitious and were as terrified as they were fascinated by spooky ideas and theories like spiritualism, the occult, and the supernatural. A case in point is this eerie tale of an unusual phenomenon that caused something of a short-lived moral panic in 19th-century England.

On the night of February 8, 1855, a peculiar series of tracks was left in a thick covering of snow that had fallen across much of the county of Devon, in the rural southwest corner of England. Each mark was vaguely horseshoe-shaped but was much smaller than a hoofprint - running around 4 inches from one tip to the other, and only around 3 inches across at the most. What's more, the tracks fell somewhat closer together than a horse's feet would, lying only a foot to a foot-and-a-half or so apart from one another.

Eerier still, however, is the fact that these "hoofmarks" were mostly all single file as if made by a person, or a two-legged creature. And strangest of all, seemingly nothing stood in their way: the trail led for mile after mile, across open fields and countryside and right through towns and villages. The tracks crossed open pastures and meadowland with ease, but also seemed to jump walls and lead on across rooftops, before leaping back down onto the ground again and continuing as before. Although reports of the incident are sketchy and varied, this one, long, seemingly unstoppable single-file line of cloven footprints stretched far across the entire county for as much as 100 miles.

Understandably, when the locals awoke on the morning of February 9, the appearance of these unusual markings in the snow outside caused something of a stir. The local people agreed that there was only one explanation: the Devil himself had visited their quiet corner of England during the night, drawn by some kind of godlessness or depravity that must surely be going on behind closed doors. These were - as they would forever become known - the Devil's Footprints.

Quite what *actually* caused this peculiar line of tracks has never truly been figured out. Some locals weren't quite so keen to assign a supernatural explanation to it. They claimed these footprints were probably instead caused by some kind of exotic animal that - unfamiliar with the worst of the British wintertime - had been spooked by the falling snow and escaped a local menagerie (collection of wild animals). One local newspaper even claimed that a kangaroo or a wallaby may have been responsible. That theory would apparently account for the tracks' ability to scale walls and buildings, given the animals' remarkable leaping abilities. No local parks or manor houses reported any missing animals from their collections at the time, however, and although kangaroos can indeed jump far, they certainly couldn't achieve the kinds of heights achieved by whatever had left these footprints.

A far more reasonable explanation was that the tracks were caused by a weight or an anchor dangling from a dislodged helium weather balloon. A balloon, caught in and pulled along by the snowstorm's updrafts and wind currents, could have easily stayed aloft while its hook-shaped counterweight dragged or bounced along the ground, leaving a trail of U-shaped markings behind it. However, no local weather stations reported any missing monitoring balloons at the time. Plus, even this more plausible theory fails to explain why the tracks appeared as footprints - with one "step" on the left, followed by another a little distance away on the right. If it really were a balloon that was responsible, then surely the track would be a single line, not a series of left-foot-right-foot paces?

To this day, the mystery of what happened that night remains unsolved.

Pigeon Post

In 1982, an Englishman named David Martin was in the middle of renovating his home - a glorious 17th-century house in the picturesque village of Bletchingley in Surrey, around 30 miles south of London - when he discovered something really quite remarkable, and very unexpected.

Stuffed up inside the house's chimney were the remains of a Second World War carrier pigeon, which had somehow expired in the chimneystack more than 40 years earlier. The pigeon, local historians supposed, had likely been flying home to England from northern France sometime around the D-Day Normandy Landings of June 1944. Perhaps, they theorized, the luckless bird had been harmed on the battlefield (carrier pigeons were common targets of enemy gunfire, given the importance of the messages they bore with them) and finally succumbed to its wounds above David's home, becoming lodged in his chimney stack as it fell to the ground. Or perhaps, an alternative theory suggested, back in the day when wood-burning open fires were more common than gas or electric-powered central heating systems, the bird was unlucky enough to find itself knocked out by the fumes from the smoking chimney and fell down the stack to its doom.

No matter *how* the pigeon happened to end up there, however, what made this tale all the more remarkable was that its cargo was still intact. Strapped to the bird's leg in a small protective metal canister was a wartime coded message. The same one the pigeon had presumably been tasked with relaying back to British Army headquarters on the English side of the Channel way back in the mid-1940s. The message, encrypted into short five-letter ciphers, read as follows:

AOAKN HVPKD FNFJU YIDDC
ROXSR DJHFP GOVFN MIAPX
PABUZ WYYNP CMPNW HJRZH
NIXKG MEMKK ONOIB AKEEQ
UAOTA RBQRH DJOFM TPZEH
LKXGH RGGHT JRZCQ FNKTQ
KLDTS GQIRU AOAKN 27 1525/6

When the discovery of the code was announced, shortly after the bird was found more than 40 years ago, the case understandably caught the attention of amateur cryptographers (code-breakers) the length and breadth of Britain. They soon set to work attempting to crack the code. None succeeded. In 2012, now 30 years after the bird's discovery (and some 70 years after its death), the case was handed over to the British Government Communications Headquarters, or GCHQ. That's an organization known and

9

respected the world over for its expert cryptanalysis, an important tool in international security and espionage. Presumably, the GCHQ experts suggested, the message was so densely encrypted because its meaning was so significant. Further, the code in which it is written was likely known by only a few individuals, and the written keys to understanding which letter stands for which, and which letters (if any) should be ignored, omitted, or recoded before deciphering them, have likely long been lost or destroyed. Ultimately, even with the best minds in the country now focused on the Bletchingley pigeon's mysterious message, the code remained unsolved.

Eventually, the story broke in the global media, and codebreakers everywhere turned their attention to the bird's mysterious cargo. Before long, GCHQ was being inundated with potential solutions sent to them from sleuths as far afield as Canada and Australia. Some of these potential breakthroughs were announced in the press, and countless newspaper reports since have deemed the code cracked and the case closed. Officially, however, to this day, GCHQ has still not accepted any of the proposed solutions, and the mystery of the Bletchingley pigeon's wartime message remains unresolved.

A Lucky Fall

There can be few things that the prospect of which terrifies every single one of us - but a plane crash, or a mid-air disaster of some sort, must surely be among them.

The fear of flying, known as aerophobia, is one of the most frequently reported fears out there. Even some of the most seasoned flyers and travelers will admit to feeling more than a little nervous during take-off and landing.

The statistics around air travel, however, speak for themselves. Improvements in aviation technology and in-flight safety features mean that the chances of an air disaster in this day and age are now quite slim - and what's more, the statistics show that even if a plane *were* to come down, incredibly, more people survive air crashes and walk free of the wreckage than perish in them. Not everyone who survives an air disaster has quite the same tale to tell, however. And surely one of the most astounding tales of air survival is that of 17-year-old Juliane Koepcke.

Koepcke was born in Peru in 1954. The daughter of German parents, who worked at the Natural History Museum in the Peruvian capital of Lima, Koepcke's childhood was spent partly at a high school in the city, and party on research expeditions with her parents deep in the Amazon rainforest.

Koepcke graduated from school in 1971 and together with her mother Maria, was booked onto a Peruvian LANSA flight on Christmas Eve that was scheduled to take her back to her parent's research station, Panguana, 350 miles west of Lima. Midway through the flight, however, Koepcke's plane flew into a huge rainforest thunderstorm. It was struck with such force by a fork of lightning that its fuselage almost instantly began to disintegrate. Within a matter of minutes, Koepcke – still strapped into her chair by her seatbelt - found herself tumbling upside down toward the rainforest canopy from a height of more than 9,000ft.

It sounds like the stuff of nightmares, but incredibly, Koepcke survived. Quite how she managed to live through being thrown from an aircraft has been the subject of decades of speculation. Some air crash experts claim that the fact that Koepcke's seat became dislodged from the aircraft with the two vacant seats on either side of hers still attached to it likely helped slow her descent, almost as a parachute would. Others claim that the storm was so tempestuous that her fall was perhaps slowed by strong updrafts and upward gusts of wind, which would have buffeted and decelerated her descent. Add to those theories the fact that she landed in an area of nearly impenetrable vegetation, which would have understandably cushioned her landing, and the mystery of Koepcke's miracle survival begins to reveal itself.

She may have survived the fall, but Koepcke's ordeal was by no means over: for the next 11 days she was forced to trek alone through the Peruvian jungle, finding food and fresh water where she could. Eventually, by following the downstream flow of a river, Koepcke arrived at a deserted logging camp, where she was able to find first aid supplies (she had broken her collarbone in the fall). She also had the foresight to clean a maggot-infected wound on her arm by flushing it with gasoline. The following day, the loggers returned to the camp, found Koepcke waiting for them, and took them with her back to the nearest town.

In the weeks and months following Koepcke's remarkable survival, it was found that, astonishingly, 11 of her fellow passengers (including her mother, Maria) had also survived the crash, and had likewise found themselves deposited by the storm, alone, in the depths of the jungle. Having not had the benefit of Koepcke's upbringing in the Amazon, however, all 11 tragically died before they could be rescued. Koepcke's story, ultimately, is the only such tale of survival against extremely narrow odds that we have.

Give Her A Hand

Given that it's one of the most famous and most popular tourist attractions in the entire United States (if not the world), there is a fairly good chance you already know the origin story of New York's Statue of Liberty.

Built out of copper, the 150 ft-tall statue - whose official name is *Liberty Enlightening the World* - was famously a gift to the US from France at the tail-end of the 19th century, as a symbol of the two nations' longstanding friendship and cooperation. Depicting an unidentified robed Roman goddess of freedom, the statue itself was designed by the French sculptor Frédéric Bartholdi (creator of the famous Bartholdi Fountain in Washington DC too). The internal supporting metal framework that holds Liberty upright was the work of the renowned engineer Gustave Eiffel (he of the Eiffel Tower, no less).

After a series of city-wide celebrations and a ticker-tape parade overseen by President Grover Cleveland, the statue was officially dedicated on October 28, 1886. But oddly, some parts - or rather, *one* part of the statue had been enjoying the sights and sounds of New York for a little longer than the rest of it.

A less well-known fact about Lady Liberty is that her torch-bearing hand and forearm arrived somewhat earlier than the rest of her. Around ten years earlier, in fact.

In 1876, the Statue of Liberty's disembodied hand arrived in New England and was put on display in Madison Square Park. The idea behind the literal gigantic gesture was a simple one: Bartholdi had arranged that he and his fellow Frenchmen would build the statue and ship it to America, so long as the Americans paid for the stone plinth on which it would stand. Unfortunately, heading toward the end of a cash-strapped 100 years of war and instability, 19th-century Americans weren't all too willing to put their hands in their pockets. Moreover, many people struggled to see the point of an enormous and somewhat expensive gesture of friendship from a nation thousands of miles away across the Atlantic Ocean.

Ultimately, in an attempt to get the financial ball rolling, Bartholdi crafted the torch-holding hand and set it across the Atlantic early, in the hopes that seeing a taste of what was to come might kickstart the donations. Fortunately, the plan worked, and the hand was immediately well received.

"Our eyes were gladdened by the actual receipt of a section of Liberty," the New York Times wrote in 1876, "consisting of one arm; with its accompanying hand of such enormous proportion that the thumbnail afforded an easy seat for the largest fat woman now in existence." All the same, it took a full six years before enough money and interest were raised to make the construction of the entire statue a realistic prospect. During all that time, from 1876 to 1882, the Statue of Liberty's giant disembodied hand sat alone in Madison Square.

A Massive Miscalculation

Leonardo da Vinci is rightly celebrated as one of the greatest artists, thinkers, and all-around geniuses ever to have lived. His work - whether technological, philosophical, mathematical, scientific, artistic, or even musical - formed one of the greatest cornerstones of the European Renaissance. Thanks to that, he is perhaps admired today more than he ever was.

But even as great a man with as great a mind as da Vinci had, even he apparently had his off days.

In one of da Vinci's many notebooks, for instance, he drew a diagram of what is now considered an early precursor of the modern armored tank, with four soldiers pictured inside a small yet heavily shielded vehicle. Going by da Vinci's visual instructions, it appears the men were intended to be able to power and direct the tank from the inside by moving a series of gears and cranks. Unfortunately, if just such a four-person man-powered tank were to be built using da Vinci's actual design, there would be a rather glaring flaw. The way he has drawn the gears in his original illustration, the two men at the front would be moving the front wheels forward, while the two men at the back would be pulling in the opposite direction, moving the tank backwards. Put another way, with all four men pushing at the same time, the vehicle would either not move at all, or simply tear itself in half!

Understandably, many people have long since come to da Vinci's defense. The diagram of the tank, they claim, was *intentionally* riddled with glaring errors so that if the design ever fell into the wrong hands, it would fail to operate effectively without da Vinci's involvement to ensure its correct construction. Alternatively, other defenders of the great man's works claim that the tank was intended to be effectively split down the middle. The two men at the front would work to haul it forward, while the two at the back would only be called into action on the off chance that the vehicle ever needed to reverse. (It seems a little unfair to have two men alone working overtime to haul such a robust contraption forward, of course, but maybe this explanation has an element of truth to it at least.)

Even da Vinci's staunchest defenders, however, can't help him get out of all his mistakes. In another of his notebooks, da Vinci explored various trigonometric and arithmetic patterns. He drew delicate pictures of the geometric nets and hollow frameworks of three-dimensional shapes and wrote out countless number sequences based on various mathematical processes. In one of these number lists, da Vinci starts at 1 and simply starts doubling each figure - 2,

4, 8, 16, 32, 64, and so on - eventually reaching the hundreds of thousands and beyond.

Unfortunately, when this page was put on display in 1940, an oversight in his workings was spotted for the very first time. Halfway down the page, da Vinci reaches the 13th stage in this doubling pattern, 4,096. Beneath it, he writes down the answer to the 14th calculation as 8,092 - exactly 100 short of the actual correct answer, 8,192. Even a mind as great as da Vinci's, it seems, sometimes forgot to carry the 1...

Tom The Turkey

Do you know what a male turkey is called?

You might be tempted to say a cock or a rooster, given the names we give to similar birds, but a male turkey is actually widely known as a tom. And according to folklore, that's a name we can credit to Benjamin Franklin.

Supposedly, Franklin was so enraged that Thomas Jefferson disliked his idea to make the humble turkey the national bird of the newly-formed United States that he championed naming the male of the birds after him as payback. The truth of that tale remains questionable, of course. Though there is at least one bizarre Tom the Turkey story that we really *do* know to be true.

In 2006, a couple living in the Chilmark on Martha's Vineyard, in Massachusetts, found an orphaned turkey chick that had been attacked and injured by a hawk. Feeling sorry for the bird, they took it home and began to rehabilitate it - treating its wounds, giving it a safe place to rest and sleep, and keeping it well-fed and watered. Although the turkey was still technically a wild bird, not a pet, they nevertheless gave him a name, Tom, and allowed him free rein to run in their yard. Unfortunately, once his wounds had healed and he was back standing, Tom took the kindness paid to him by his rescuers a little too far.

Before long, Tom had become the terror of his small neighborhood. Although he continued acting kindly to his adoptive parents, he treated others in quite the opposite way - chasing and attacking children, running after neighbors as they walked home, and even forcing them to dive for cover in their cars. Eventually, enough was enough. One day, a luckless delivery woman who had a parcel for one of Tom's neighbors called animal control when he attacked her. Two armed officers quickly responded to reports of a wild and dangerous turkey roaming the quiet streets of Chilmark. At first, Tom kept the officers at bay, even forcing one of them to take cover on the roof of their vehicle. Eventually, however, Tom's luck ran out and when his behavior became too unruly to be tolerated, the officers chased him down, and Tom was killed.

In the aftermath, Tom's adoptive father was so horrified that he scuffled with the responding officers and was sent to jail for assault. The entire sorry affair soon proved a scandalous *cause célèbre* (a famous case that causes a big reaction). Tom became a talking point all around the world, as media commentators discussed the apparent heavy-handedness of the controllers' response.

Even after his untimely death, it seemed, Tom, the Turkey remained something of a controversial figure...

Back From The Dead

Here's an extraordinary statistic that sounds too wild to be true, but that is - as far as biologists and ecologists can work out, at least - entirely accurate. Throughout the history of the Earth, more than 99% of all the animal species to have ever walked our planet are now extinct.

At first glance, that seems impossible: in 2011, scientists calculated that the world is currently home to over 8.7 million different animal species (including our own!). So, the idea that this could be a mere fraction of a single percent of the historical total seems way off the mark. But those self-same scientists also estimated that the total number of species ever to have lived on our planet must now number in the region of 4 *billion* - of which those alive today truly do represent a small fraction.

At the opposite end of this extraordinary calculation is surely one of the most unlikely zoological icons imaginable. It's a creature thought to have long gone the way of the dinosaurs, but which was rediscovered a little over 100 years ago living perfectly well in the bottom of the ocean.

The coelacanth is a large, eight-finned fish with mottled grey and white scales, growing to a length of around 8 ft or so. The Earth's fossil record suggests the creature first emerged sometime around 410 million years ago. That makes it a contemporary companion of the likes of Tyrannosaurus Rex and the dinosaur world's latest Pterosaurs. For decades, it was presumed the coelacanth had died out alongside its dinosaur contemporaries, sometime around the late Cretaceous period. At least, that was until 1938, when a live coelacanth was unexpectedly found in the oceanic waters off the east coast of South Africa.

Since then, zoologists have gone on to find a relatively robust population of coelacanths living in the Indian Ocean - as well as two smaller subspecies populations, one off the coast of Africa's Comoros Islands, north of Madagascar, and second on the other side of the ocean, off the west coast of Indonesia.

Incredibly, the rediscovery of the coelacanth meant that it effectively vanished from our fossil record - and was, as far as we knew, extinct - for more than 65 million years! That makes it the most extreme example of a zoological phenomenon known as the Lazarus effect, in which a creature thought to have long left our world is found once again in the wild and "resurrected," like Lazarus.

Did You Know?

Seven More Animals Once Thought to Be Extinct

○ **TAKAHE**

Found in the swamps and wetlands of New Zealand, the takahe is a character-filled flightless water bird with shimmering bottle-green plumage, and a thick, bright red, wedge-shaped bill. It was officially assumed to be extinct in 1898, but exactly 50 years later a small population was rediscovered in the New Zealand wilderness in 1948. Conservation projects ever since have steadily brought the bird back from the very edge of extinction, and although it is still listed as endangered - and officially "nationally vulnerable" in New Zealand - there are now approximately 400 individual birds, with the population growing by around a tenth every year.

○ **NEW GUINEA BIG-EARED BAT**

Also known as the Papuan big-eared bat, the New Guinea big-eared bat was presumed to have gone extinct way back in 1890 when the last known individuals were seen in the wild. That was until as recently as 2012 when a female bat caught by researchers on the south of the island of New Guinea was indeed found to be a big-eared bat - the first for more than 120 years. The bats have since been found at a second location, further down the coast, leading to hopes that a breeding population exists somewhere in the wild linking these two final strongholds together.

○ GREEN BROADBILL

The green broadbill is a brilliant bright green perching bird native to the forests of central Indonesia Malaysia, Myanmar, and Thailand, on the islands of Sumatra, Borneo, and the Malay Peninsula, in lowland forests of broadleaved evergreen and lower Montane rainforest. It was thought to have gone extinct due to habitat loss in the early 1940s before a small population was rediscovered in the summer of 2021.

○ MILLER'S LANGUR

Miller's langur - also known as the grizzled langur, given its pale gray facial fur—is one of the world's rarest primates. In fact, the creature is so rare that its extinction was declared several times in the scientific community, most recently in 2004. In 2012, however, researchers working in the forests of Borneo rediscovered a tiny surviving population of Miller's langur, based on evidence from remote camera traps left in the jungle. Incredibly, the creature is so scarce that it was difficult to work out precisely what type of monkey the cameras had spotted as there are so few photographs of Miller's langur in the zoological record.

○ NIGHT PARROT

The Australian night parrot is a ground-dwelling parrot native to the sparse grasslands of the Australian Outback. The problem is, the Outback is so enormously vast and hostile an environment—and the night parrot is so seldom seen outside of patches of thick undergrowth—that it is notoriously difficult to assess its population figures. For a long time, it was believed to be extinct. The last reliable sighting of a night parrot was in 1912, but reports of flocks of the birds have been growing since the late 1970s, and it now seems likely a small, yet sadly declining population of approximately 10 - 20, still exists somewhere in the vast central desert of Australia.

○ GREATER BERMUDA LAND SNAIL

The greater Bermuda land snail, native only to the island of Bermuda, was already critically endangered when a zoological survey failed to find a single individual in the late 1970s. Later surveys in the 1980s, 1990s, and early 2000s appeared to confirm that the creature had indeed gone extinct - until a small group of snails was found living, of all places, among the trash in an alleyway in the island's capital, Hamilton, in 2019. After the snail rediscovery, some were taken to the Zoological Society of London and Chester Zoo in the UK. A breeding programme resulted in 18,000 Greater Land snails being brought back to Bermuda in 2019. They have been placed on five Castle islands (including Nonsuch) and are thriving.

○ **MACHU PICCHU ARBOREAL CHINCHILLA RAT**
The ancient inhabitants of the Andean city of Machu Picchu would have known all about these arboreal chinchilla rats. Unfortunately, just as the city itself was eventually abandoned and fell into ruin, so too did the chinchilla rat. Until as recently as the early 2000s, all we knew about these creatures was the evidence from the local fossil record, as it was thought the rats went extinct sometime around the early 1500s. However, photographs of a live specimen spotted in the jungles around Machu Picchu were published in 2020, hauling the arboreal chinchilla rat out of extinction after more than five centuries. While officially classified as extinct, there's a good chance that the Machu Picchu arboreal chinchilla rats are still hiding out in the cloud forests of Peru.

Moonshot

There's still an awful lot we don't know about how the natural world functions, of course, but compared to a century or so ago, our understanding has taken leaps and bounds. Our ancestors, however, weren't quite so lucky.

Before modern technology made our world smaller and better connected than ever before, our understanding of the world was based on what we could see around us in the here and now. And that meant that one facet of the natural world that we scarcely give a second thought to today was, for a long time, a complete mystery: the world-spanning migration of animals.

When you think about it, migration is truly astonishing. Driven by the changing of the seasons, some birds, animals, and even insects set off on impossibly long journeys around our planet. The tiny Arctic tern, for instance, travels from the Arctic to the Antarctic and back each year, to complete an annual migration of around 44,000 miles - not bad for a bird with scarcely a one-foot wingspan, and that weighs less than 5 ounces.

Eastern populations of North America's monarch butterfly, meanwhile, travel more than 3,000 miles every autumn from the Atlantic coast of the US down to their overwintering sites in Mexico. And in the seas, a leatherback turtle was recently found to have traveled more than 12,000 miles from one side of the Pacific Ocean to the other, from its home off the coast of Oregon to its breeding site among the islands of Indonesia.

Today, what we know about migrations like these is based on decades of observation and fieldwork. It can now be proved using the likes of remote tracking devices, satellite technology, and global positioning systems. Back in the day, however, things weren't quite so easy to explain. People would simply see the seasonal animals around them suddenly disappear, before reappearing several months later as if nothing had happened. As a result, early naturalists and thinkers concocted all manner of outlandish theories to explain where migratory animals went.

For a long time, for instance, it was thought that migratory birds like swallows and martins hibernated underwater during the colder winter months. According to this ancient theory, the reason we see so many of them skimming across the surface of lakes and ponds during the summertime is that they have only just returned from below the water's surface.

Other birds were once believed to "transmogrify" - spontaneously transforming themselves into other species for part of the year, before magically going back to their former selves when the time is right. The Greek philosopher

Aristotle, for instance, believed that redstarts, a red-breasted member of the thrush family, turned into robins during the winter months.

And in the 17th century, the British naturalist Charles Morton proposed perhaps the most bizarre theory of all. Morton claimed the reason certain species of birds disappear during the winter is that they are no longer on the planet! His theory - backed up by his observations of high-flying V-shaped flocks of geese - was the migratory animals fled to the Moon when the cold weather set in.

Back in Morton's day, of course, not only did we not fully understand animal migration, but we also had no idea of the realities of space, nor the true size of the distance between the Earth and the Moon - roughly 239,000 miles. That's enough to make even an Arctic tern think twice!

Zombie Fungus

There are lots of different theories explaining where our grisly idea of the zombie first came from.

One of the most popular is that zombies originate in the eerie voodoo culture of the Caribbean. Supposedly, one of the ancient practices among voodoo practitioners involved sealing a living person in a wooden casket beneath the ground, supposedly so that they could commune with the deceased. Once their ordeal was over and the person was dug back up, their prolonged time in the darkness and the unavoidable lack of oxygen beneath the earth would often leave them in an eerie stumbling stupor. This eventually led to folklore and stories of the walking dead.

Whether that tale is true or not is debatable - but elsewhere in the world, it's fair to say zombies aren't entirely fictional...

Cordyceps is the name of a vast genus of fungus, of which more than 600 different individual species have now been described. Like many fungi, the *Cordyceps* reproduce by wafting clouds of microscopic spores into the air. And if one of these spores happens to invade the body of a luckless passing insect or invertebrate, it quickly begins to take over its new host's brain, gradually changing it into a zombie-like walking corpse.

The *Cordyceps* spore is all but pre-programmed to find its way into the insect's brain, where it slowly begins replacing its soft tissues with its own. In doing so, the *Cordyceps* effectively takes control of the insect's body. It begins to compel it forward and upward, forcing it to brainlessly climb as high as possible - up the stems of plans or the trunks of trees - above the forest floor. Eventually, the braindead creature no longer has enough of its own neural system intact to function any further and grinds to a halt. It's at this point that the *Cordyceps* moves to the next stage in its life cycle, and begins to produce long mushroom-like tendrils that erupt from its control center in the host's head. Eventually, these new fungal bodies begin to produce new clouds of *Cordyceps* spores, which rain down onto the ground below, ready to infect a new host and take over its body with its zombie-like powers once again.

It all sounds a little too grim to possibly be real, but the *Cordyceps* is nevertheless science fact, not science fiction. This gruesome tale has an extraordinary twist, however. As grisly and as stomach-churning as the *Cordyceps'* life cycle may be, the dried bodies of *Cordyceps*-infected insects are today popularly used in certain forms of Eastern and alternative medicine. Yes, still with the fungal stems attached, growing from their heads!

Although many of the purported medical benefits of the cordyceps fungus are yet to be confirmed by science, some studies have so far suggested that consuming it may help to mitigate some of the symptoms of type-2 diabetes, improve the body's oxygen use during aerobic exercise, and may even inhibit the growth of certain cancers and tumors. It may be one of the natural world's most gruesome beings, but the *Cordyceps* may yet prove one of our natural saviors.

Total Tyranny

Did you know that your idea of Tyrannosaurus rex is probably a little misguided?

When we imagine a T-rex, most of us probably conjure up a terrifying image of a gigantic bloodthirsty predator, with beady eyes, long fangs, and a monstrous roar. But understandably, much of what we know about the behavior of dinosaurs is conjectural, that is, it's just guessing. So, a lot of what many of us pictures when we think of a T-rex may well be wrong.

For one thing, some paleontologists now believe that Tyrannosaurus rex was not a hunter, but a scavenger. Rather than pursuing and killing other dinosaurs in cold blood, it's possible that the T-rex merely picked up the scraps left behind by smaller, faster, leaner, and more successful predatory dinosaurs—like the man-sized Utahraptor (the true inspiration for *Jurassic Park's* velociraptors) and the approximately 30-ft-long Baryonyx. If that theory were correct, then the larger tyrannosaurs were the prehistoric world's vultures - wandering the plains and jungles looking for what remains of other dinosaurs' kills they could find.

The theory that T-rex was a scavenger rather than a predator has been the subject of paleontological debate for decades now, and it is by no means universally accepted. But in 2014, a remarkable dinosaur discovery in the deserts of the western United States once more turned our idea of Tyrannosaurus rex on its head.

At a site in Grand Staircase-Escalante National Monument in southern Utah, researchers from the US Bureau of Land Management stumbled across the remains of not one, but an entire group of tyrannosaurs. At first, they found just a single ankle bone, but as they began to excavate it from the earth, the bones of a further four dinosaurs, all of the same species, were uncovered.

Based on their size, the researchers estimated that the group comprised just one single adult, an adolescent or subadult, and three smaller juveniles. Further research concluded that all five creatures died at the same time in a single cataclysmic event - most likely a flood or a mudslide. The discovery suggested the group was effectively an extended family, and may well have been just a handful of individuals from an even larger related group, the majority of which managed to escape the same fate.

Rather than being merely a solitary scavenger, it's possible that the tyrannosaurs were the complete opposite. Ultimately, they may have been pack hunters that worked together to bring down prey they might not be able to handle individually, much like wolves or lions do today. Again, it is a theory that is not without controversy, and proof of T-rex hunting packs remains vanishingly rare in the fossil record. Nevertheless, the Utah discovery offered a tantalizing glimpse of what may well have been the day-to-day life of one of the world's most iconic and most terrifying creatures.

Dead Serious

Lots of places around the world are subject to bizarre and unexpected laws.

For instance, it is popularly said to be illegal to look at a moose from a plane in Alaska. It is illegal to feed pigeons in Venice (and, since 2003, in London's famous Trafalgar Square too). No one can enter the British Houses of Parliament wearing a suit of armor, either. And in Scotland, an age-old legal statute still says that it is against the law to ride a Highland cow while intoxicated.

Of all the world's most unusual laws and regulations, however, perhaps the strangest of all is enforced in the isolated Arctic town of Longyearbyen in the far north of Norway. There, it is quite literally against the law to die.

Longyearbyen is famous for being one of the world's most northerly permanent settlements (and it remains the most northerly town on the planet with a population of more than 1,000 people). Located on the rocky and snow-covered island of Svalbard, far inside the Arctic Circle, temperatures in the town regularly drop to below −22°F, and seldom rise above freezing for eight months out of the year.

It is this perishingly cold climate that is at least partly responsible for Longyearbyen's notoriously unusual approach to the legality of death. With the ground in and around the town frozen solid for much of the year, burials are simply not an option. People who do happen to die in the town can be cremated (on the Norwegian mainland) and have their

39

canister of their ashes buried in the town, but *not* their bodies. What's more, any unfortunate local who is unlucky enough to fall morbidly or terminally ill is, by law, required to be transported to the mainland for any necessary or subsequent end-of-life care.

If all of this sounds bizarrely uncompromising, there is a good reason for the town taking such a no-nonsense approach to death. In 1918, during the Spanish flu pandemic that affected much of the human world, dozens of Longyearbyen locals succumbed to the virus. As it was long before the current regulations were enacted, they were buried in the town. More than 30 years later, however, it was found in 1950 that the bodies of these flu victims had not yet begun to decompose, even after three decades in the ground. Preserved by permafrost, they had instead remained almost entirely intact - a discovery that soon raised worrisome questions about whether the deadly microorganism that had killed them had also been preserved in ice too.

In an ever-warming climate, the prospect of the Spanish flu re-emerging and decimating the town once more became a very real threat. As a result, it was off the back of this grisly discovery that the law in Longyearbyen was changed in the mid-1900s. Although the precise wording of the law does not outlaw dying *itself* in the town, locals are nevertheless forbidden from being buried. They are also encouraged, if possible, to move elsewhere toward the end of their natural life.

Forest Folly

Before metal-framed ships powered by coal and steam became the norm at the beginning of the last century, wood was understandably the material of choice for the world's seafarers and explorers. Building a ship, however, is no mean feat. Naval historians have estimated that the construction of a typical 110-rank gunship, of the kind much used in Europe and North America in the 18th century, would have required the timber of somewhere in the region of 4,000 individual oak trees - that's around 40 hectares (98.8422 acres) of felled woodland.

Building a *single* ship, moreover, is one thing. Building a fleet of ships is another.

If your country were at war - at a time when battles may well be waged at sea, or when troops may need to be transported across the open ocean to fight in far-off lands - it may well have been necessary to produce multiple vessels simultaneously. But that posed something of a problem: trees are slow growing. What's more, the strongest timber often had to be hewn (chopped) from the oldest and longest-established trees and forests. Under wartime conditions, ultimately, many countries and their naval forces once risked using up their national supply of suitable timber faster than their forests and woodlands could naturally replenish it.

In 17th-century France, however, one man came up with an ingenious and ambitious project to offset that risk.

In 1670, Jean-Baptiste Colbert - the First Minister of the French State under King Louis XIV - realized that the French navy may well run out of trees and timber before a full national armada (fleet of warships), robust enough to defend France's coastline and its territories around the globe, could be built. As a result, he proposed the planting of a gigantic oak forest - essentially, a 40-square-mile national park - right in the center of the country.

Known as the Forest of Tronçais (after the oak or *tronce* trees that are grown there), the plan was that Colbert's trees would be left to mature, untouched, for the next 200 years. This would ensure a future store of timber that would see France and her navy right through the 19th and 20th centuries. As this was to be a custom-built forest, Colbert ingeniously arranged for its high-value oak trees to be intermixed with beech, larch, pine, and hornbeam. As they grew straighter and more rapidly than the oaks, they would effectively form a natural framework or scaffolding around them, encouraging the oaks to grow more upright and so keeping their wood strong and free of knots and tangles.

Colbert, it seemed, had thought of every possible eventuality. Except, that is, the dawn of the metal ship.

42

As naval technology improved, the slower, heavier, wind-reliant timber-framed sailing ships of the past gradually fell out of fashion. They were replaced with the sleeker, faster, more rapidly constructed metal steamships of the modern world. Colbert's forest of premium shipbuilding timber, ultimately, was no longer needed.

There was a silver lining to the failure of his plan, however: the Forest of Tronçais is now one of the most important areas of woodland in all of western Europe. As well as being an important refuge for wildlife of all shapes and sizes, it comprises one of the world's largest stands of oak trees. It may never have been used as Colbert had intended it to, but in ecological terms, it has remained just as valuable today as it always was.

Absolutely Shattered

The medieval king Charles VI of France rose to the French throne at the age of just 11, following the death of his father, Charles V, in September 1380.

Initially, the young king proved popular with his court and the French people alike. Despite his youth and inexperience, he arranged a learned council of advisors and family members - including his uncles, the Dukes of Burgundy, Anjou, Berry, and Bourbon - to help run the country alongside him. The early years of his reign were ultimately stable and judicious, and as Charles grew into a handsome and capable adult, it seemed to all of France that they were in truly safe hands. At the age of 20, Charles emancipated himself from his uncles' care and regency. He began to rule the country solo.

All was going well until the summer of 1392, when Charles, now 23, instigated a series of military excursions against the rival Duchy of Brittany, in the northern corner of France. Midway through a particularly decisive battle, Charles was reportedly struck with a sudden fit of delirium or insanity. In his confused state, he turned around and began attacking his own men. The curious incident shook the confidence of his court, but as it appeared to be only an isolated affair, Charles was permitted to continue his reign.

A year later, however, a disastrous event at the king's palace again shook France's confidence in the young king. A debauched ball descended into chaos when a flaming torch set alight to a group of dancers' costumes. Charles was once more placed back in the care of his uncles and their regency. This proved one setback too many, and Charles retreated into isolation and, eventually, a bizarre form of madness. The king became utterly and debilitatingly obsessed with the groundless belief that his body was made of glass.

One wrong move, the king believed, and he would shatter to pieces and die. To prevent his untimely death, he consequently began to dress in layer upon layer of dense cushioned fabric and would spend much of his day sitting perfectly motionless on his throne. If he did have to move for whatever reason, he would don a specially tailored suit that contained supporting iron struts to hold his body as upright and as stable as possible. This was to avoid his supposed glass organs bursting and rupturing through his skin.

As the king's madness grew worse, so too did his reign. Charles' inability to lead or organize his armies led to military disaster after military disaster, eventually culminating in France's devastating loss to England at the Battle of Agincourt in 1415. As part of the postwar settlement, Charles was forced to sign a treaty disinheriting his son's right to the throne, in favor of his future son-in-law, the English king Henry V.

Despite Charles' ailing health, bizarrely, King Henry died before him. As a result, Charles' son's rightful claim to the throne was later restored and France was eventually able to recoup many of the disastrous losses of Charles' reign in victory in the Hundred Years' War. But it was due to sheer chance, not Charles' kingship or leadership, that circumstances had fallen this way. Consequently, Charles the Beloved, as he had once been known at the start of his reign, has since gone down in history under the nickname Charles the Mad.

Did You Know?

Seven More Mad Monarchs

○ **PRINCESS ALEXANDRA AMELIE**

Amazingly, Charles VI wasn't the only European royal to believe their body was made of glass. Princess Alexandra Amelie was the daughter of King Ludwig I of Bavaria. In her early twenties, in the mid-1840s, she became obsessed with the delusion that as a child she had eaten an entire grand piano made of glass that now sat inside her body, still in one piece! The slightest touch or quick movement, she believed, would shatter the piano to pieces and kill her instantly.

○ **THE ZHENGDE EMPEROR OF CHINA**

One of the most notorious rulers of China's famous Ming dynasty, the Zhengde Emperor ruled from 1491–1521. During that time, he became known more for his capricious cruelty than his madness (at one point infamously sentencing one of his court eunuchs "to death by slow slicing"). Bizarre tales and literary records from the time of Zhengde's reign, however, have led to suggestions that the emperor's cruelty was at least partly caused by mental derangement. According to one such story, the emperor once ate a bowl of cheaply made rice gruel because he thought it was a bowl of boiled pearls.

○ HOLY ROMAN EMPEROR RUDOLF II

Leader of the Holy Roman Empire for a full six decades, from 1552–1612, Rudolf II was widely known as an intellectual and tirelessly inquisitive monarch. He financially supported many of the greatest thinkers of his day (including the astronomer Tycho Brahe) and assembled one of the most remarkable royal menageries of the European Renaissance (which at one point included a live dodo bird). Between his bouts of enthusiastic learning, however, the king was known to retreat into deep and unpredictable bouts of melancholy. During these times he would withdraw to his private chambers alone, often for weeks on end. When he was required to attend court during one of his more melancholic episodes, the king would either refuse to speak at all or only speak in a barely audible whisper to those closest to him. This left the rest of his court entirely clueless as to what he was demanding!

○ CALIGULA

Perhaps the most famously crazed ruler in history, throughout his 29-year reign the Roman emperor Caligula became known for his cruelty, his love of luxury, and, allegedly, his utter madness. Given the stories about him demanding his troops collect seashells in their helmets and commissioning a two-mile floating bridge just so he could gallop his horse across it, Caligula's reputation as a mad monarch is arguably well deserved. Having ordered the construction of a grand palace in which his horse could live, moreover, Caligula began making arrangements for his horse to be made a city consul - but was assassinated before his final ludicrous plan could be enacted.

KING GEORGE III

England's longest-ruling king, George III spent much of the final decades of his 60-year reign, 1760-1801, suffering from utterly debilitating bouts of madness. He was lost in empty stupors sparked by his physicians' countless attempts to cure him of his malady. Although the cause of the king's madness remains unclear, countless stories about its many peculiar manifestations fill the history books. According to one of the most famous tales of "the madness of King George," he once shook hands with a willow tree in his garden because he thought it was the King of Prussia.

KING CHRISTIAN VII OF DENMARK

King Christian reigned in Denmark for almost 40 years until his death in 1808. For much of that time, however, he was king in name only. He suffered near-endless bouts of melancholy, mood swings, hallucinations, and paranoia, and is even said to have eventually spiraled into devastating periods of self-mutilation. Modern reassessments of the king's malady have suggested he likely suffered from some undiagnosed form of schizophrenia.

○ KING FAROUK OF EGYPT

There is a fine line between eccentricity and madness, of course, and the deposed King Farouk of Egypt - who came to the throne as recently as 1936 - supposedly straddled it. On the more whimsical and eccentric side of things, Farouk is known to have demanded that he only ever drive or be driven in red cars, while simultaneously banning anyone else in the country from owning one. On the more deranged side of things, however, he is known to have suffered from both mysophobia (a morbid dislike of anything dirty) and kleptomania (addiction to stealing). According to one tale, the king reportedly once stole Winston Churchill's watch!

Treehouse Of Horror

Every child wants a treehouse at some point in their life - but surely nobody will ever end up with anything like the extraordinary 97ft-tall treehouse that was built by American eccentric Horace Burgess in the Tennessee town of Crossville in the late 1990s.

Known as The Minister's House, Burgess spent 14 years constructing a treehouse so grand that it was officially recognized as the world's largest by the *Guinness Book of Records*. Straddling six gigantic oak trees and held together by a quarter of a million nails, the treehouse had ten floors - with a combined floor space of more than 30,000 square ft - and housed more than 80 rooms, including several bedrooms, classrooms, a kitchen, and even a miniature indoor basketball court.

A single snaking staircase linked all ten stories together, while the entire structure was encircled by a suitably Tennessee-style wraparound porch. Having claimed to have been given planning permission by God to construct the house, Burgess repaid the divine favor by finding room inside his extraordinary structure for several places of worship. This included a pew-lined chapel, a giant crucifix, a hand-carved wooden Bible, and even a preacher's pulpit.

Understandably, the Minister's House proved something of a tourist trap, and dozens of visitors would turn up each day to climb inside and wander around the world's biggest treehouse. Unfortunately, divine permission is not legally binding in the state of Tennessee. In 2012, the local fire marshals in Crossville became concerned about the Minister's House's safety and demanded it should be closed to the public.

Their concerns appear to have been well placed because, in 2019, a fire broke out at the treehouse. The entire structure - now the result of more than a quarter of a century of work - burnt to the ground in less than 15 minutes. Local firemen reported that the blaze was so intense that they had to park their trucks more than 500 yards away from the fire. By the time they gained access to the site, nothing was left of Burgess' treehouse apart from smoldering rubble. The cause of the fire remains unknown to this day.

Drum It Again, Sam

It remains one of the most famous lines in cinema history. It's also never actually spoken in the movie.

Cinematic folklore has it that in 1942's film classic *Casablanca*, Richard "Rick" Blaine (played by an Oscar-nominated Humphrey Bogart) turns to the piano player in his ex-pats' bar, the *Café Américain* in Morocco, and casually demands, "Play it again, Sam." In fact, Bogart's line in the movie is simply, "Play it, Sam."

Somewhat earlier in the film, Rick's love interest Ilsa Lund (played by Ingrid Bergman, in one of her earliest screen appearances) comes close to muttering the now famous line herself, when she asks the pianist to, "Play it once, Sam." But neither star - nor indeed anyone else in the movie, for that matter—utters the line that has since become immortalized, "Play it again, Sam." So, it seems one of the most famous lines in movie history is really nothing more than a misquote, popularly handed on from film fanatic to film fanatic for decade after decade.

And while we're busy busting myths about one of Hollywood's greatest-ever movies, we might as well ruin one more enduring image: Sam himself never actually *played* it at all. In fact, the real Sam wasn't even a pianist, but a drummer!

The role of Sam the pianist in Rick's café was taken on by the American actor, singer, and musician Arthur "Dooley" Wilson. Wilson started his showbiz career in the mid-1920s, initially as the drummer and bandleader of a show group that had moderate success touring the UK and Europe between the First and Second World Wars. Based fully back in America in the early 1930s, Wilson switched from his earlier musical career to take up acting and appeared in a string of supporting roles on Broadway before making the move to movies in 1939.

Having signed with Paramount Pictures, Dooley had to be lent to Warner Brothers to appear in *Casablanca*. Warner wanted Dooley for the role of Sam, and so a deal was struck early in 1942 that allowed Dooley to work on the picture for seven weeks, earning a not-inconsiderable wage of $500 for each week's work. In casting a professional drummer to play a pianist, however, there was an obvious problem: the actor they had cast to play Sam, couldn't actually "play it" at all.

To get around the issue, Dooley merely mimed his piano playing in Rick's café, while a professional pianist off-camera played *As Time Goes By* so he could sing along to it. Once filming was finishing, a clearer recording of the song was dubbed over the top of the scene, and Dooley went down in history as playing perhaps Hollywood's most famous pianist -despite never actually playing the piano at all!

A Photograph To Remember

In 1985, a large metal chest containing more than 42,000 photographs, photographic plates, and photographic negatives was discovered in the Irish capital of Dublin. The discovery was made in the basement of a Jesuit provincial house, which is a residence for Jesuit priests.

Among the hoard of images was a somewhat worn out, unsuspecting-looking photographic album, which may well have been ignored or even thrown away given its tatty appearance. Luckily for us - and luckily for maritime history, for that matter - the album was salvaged from the photographic scrap heap. Inside it were some of the most important photographs of the 20th century: the last known photographs taken on board the doomed '*White Star*' ocean liner, the RMS *Titanic*.

The photographs were taken by taken in April 1912 by Frank Hegarty Browne (who would later go on to be ordained at the Jesuit house as Father Francis Browne). Born in Cork, in southern Ireland, in 1880, Browne was 32 years old when he was gifted a trip on the *Titanic* by his uncle. He joined the ship at Southampton, on the south coast of England, but his ticket was not a transatlantic one (going across to America). So, after a brief stop at Cherbourg in northern France, Browne alighted at Queenstown (now Cobh, in County Cork) and returned to Dublin, leaving the ship to continue on its ill-fated voyage without him.

When the *Titanic* sank early in the morning of 15 April 1912, the importance of Browne's final pictures soon became clear. Before long, Browne was inundated with requests from journalists and reporters from all across Europe and North America to use the images. In the days and weeks that followed, Browne's snapshots were printed and circulated in newspapers all over the world.

Among his many pictures were the last known photograph of the ship's captain Edward Smith; the only known photograph of the ship's onboard gymnasium; and an image of the interior of Browne's own cabin on the *Titanic*, number 37A. When the ship was found lying in two pieces on the bed of the Atlantic Ocean in 1985, it was found to have torn apart right through where Browne had been staying.

With his life now so closely intertwined with the sinking of the *Titanic*, Browne went on to make a career as a public speaker, alongside his work in the church. He gave lectures and talks on the *Titanic* and his experiences on board for much of the rest of his life. He died in Dublin in 1960 at the age of 80, whereupon his vast collection of photographs - including those he had used in his talks - were placed in storage and forgotten.

Thankfully, they did not remain hidden for long, however, and now provide us with an extraordinary first-hand glimpse into one of the most infamous events in modern history.

Five Alive

It's a gesture that seems all but commonplace these days and can be seen everywhere from your local CrossFit gym to Olympic stadiums. But have you ever wondered why we *high-five* someone when either we or they succeed at something?

There is (as always with these things) one supposed origin story that has proved more popular than any other. According to legend, the high five gesture was the brainchild of Lamont Sleets Sr., a US Army veteran who served in the 1st Battalion, 5th Infantry, during the Vietnam War. Thanks to its numerical designation, Sleets' army unit became popularly known as the Five. After the war, Sleets and his fellow Fives would still regularly meet to catch up and reminisce - and would supposedly greet one another at Sleets' home with a friendly slapping together of their open palms. And so, the high-five was born.

Except, unfortunately, it wasn't. The story of Sleets' involvement in the creation of the high five is sheer fabrication, concocted in the early 2000s by the organizers of an unofficial holiday known as "National High-Five Day." To raise awareness of their day, the organizers sent out a press release crediting Sleets with the gesture's creation.

This remarkable tale of a decorated army vet's impromptu gesture that had taken the world by storm proved instantly popular online. But, alas, that didn't stop it from being a total lie.

So, if it wasn't Sleets' invention, where did the high-five come from?

The second most popular explanation - which has the benefit of being at least partly verifiable - credits the high five to two teammates on the Los Angeles Dodgers baseball team. In 1977, LA outfielder Dusty Baker scored his 30th home run of the season. As he celebrated the landmark achievement, Baker was greeted at the home plate by his teammate, Glenn Burke, who was standing with his hand in the air. Not knowing how best to receive Burke's congratulations, Baker slapped his open hand against Burke's, and embraced him - and thus, the high-five really was born.

The spur-of-the-moment gesture soon caught on among Baker's and Burke's other teammates, as well as Dodgers fans and staff at the stadium. Before long, it had been given a name - the high-five - and fans were able to purchase official "LA Dodgers High Five" T-shirts from vendors in and around Dodger Stadium.

A Tale Of Skulduggery

As the First World War drew to a close, a peace treaty was needed to ensure that a line could at long last be drawn under the brutal conflict.

Hundreds of diplomats and envoys from across the globe convened at the Palace of Versailles in 1919 and together thrashed out a bewilderingly lengthy treaty. It comprised many hundreds of clauses of annexes, outlining in minute detail precisely what reparations were to be imposed on Germany and its fellow Axis forces. And, amid days of chaotic negotiations, many countries took the opportunity to enforce some truly surprising demands.

One such clause was the stipulation that as part of their country's wartime reparations, the German pharmaceutical company Bayer should give up their trademark claim to the names of the drugs Aspirin and Heroin. The latter (even more bizarrely) was at the time used worldwide as a cough suppressant. The pharmaceutical clause handed both trademarks over in part to the allied nations of the United Kingdom, France, and Russia (as well as, later, to the United States). It simultaneously demanded that Bayer henceforth ship one-quarter of all the aspirin it produced to the Allied nations.

As peculiar as that particular stipulation may be, however, even that is arguably not the most bizarre penalty imposed on Germany at Versailles. For that, we need to head several decades further back in time.

Chief Mkwawa was a leader of the Wahehe people of Tanganyika (modern-day Tanzania) in the late 1800s. At the time, Mkwawa's country was under the colonial control of Germany, and he was one of a handful of local Tanzanian leaders who led a fierce rebellion against local German rule. His campaign was so successful that in 1891, German leaders in East Africa placed a bounty on Mkwawa's head. To offset the risk of his life falling into the colonizers' hands, Mkwawa is said to have taken his own life. But even that, it seems, was not enough to end Germany's uncompromisingly harsh rule of his country.

As a way of sending a twisted message to intimidate the Wahehe tribespeople - and thereby prevent any future uprisings - when Mkwawa's body was found, the German colonists had it decapitated, and his skull placed on a plinth in a house in the city of Bagamoyo. At the outbreak of the First World War, the German leaders in Tanganyika were instantly recalled to Europe and, outrageously, took Mkwawa's skull back to Berlin with them.

After the war, one of the many diplomats involved in drawing up the Treaty of Versailles was a British colonial administrator based in East Africa named Horace Byatt. He lobbied his fellow Allies to include the return of Mkwawa's skull to the Wahehe people as one of the clauses in the treaty. This was both as a way of proving to the Tanzanians that German rule of the area had indeed been crushed and also as a means of not-so-subtly persuading them to accept the rule of the British Empire instead, which had taken over control of Germany's East Africa territories.

Initially, the demand was deemed too bizarre and distracting an issue to be included in the treaty. Minutes (records) from the many diplomatic meetings at Versailles show that the impact of the skull's return to Tanzania was deemed "hardly sufficient" for its inclusion "in the venerable peace treaty" being thrashed out. Once the issue had been raised, however, it caught the imagination of another British envoy, Colonial Secretary Viscount Milner, who likewise supported the skull's return. Eventually, he was able to successfully lobby for it to be included under Article 246 of the Treaty of Versailles, which dealt with the return and redistribution of German-held items of artistic and cultural significance.

The clause originally stipulated that the skull be returned to the Wahehe people within six months of the signing of the treaty. However, such were the circumstances in Germany immediately after the First World War (and then heading

62

into the Second World War) that in the end, Mkwawa was not sent home for another 35 years.

Toadally Unbelievable

In 2010, an article was published in the academic *Journal of Zoology* that claimed something truly remarkable. It said that toads may be able to predict earthquakes, often several days before they actually take place!

The research behind the paper was based on observations of toad behavior in the lead-up to an earthquake measuring 5.9 on the Richter scale that struck the town of L'Aquila, in central Italy, in 2009. More than 300 people were killed in the quake, which remains one of the deadliest ever to have struck 21st-century Europe.

In the aftermath of the disaster, local zoologists began to report that a colony of toads they had been observing suddenly and unexplainedly deserted their mating site, a shallow pool roughly 50 miles outside the earthquake's epicenter. This occurred 72 hours before the tremor itself struck.

The scientists who had been observing the toads weren't interested at first in the creatures' apparent prognosticating (predicting) abilities. Instead, they had been studying the effects of the cycles of the moon on the toads' mating behavior. Each night during the study period, the researchers had gone out under cover of darkness to count the number of active toads in the pool, which typically amounted to several dozen. But one night - exactly three days before the earthquake - the scientists arrived at the site to find the pool entirely deserted.

It was not uncommon for mating numbers to drop in response to the likes of temperature changes or heavy wind or rain. However, with no obvious reason for the toads' disappearance, the researchers were baffled - and remained so when the animals still had not returned the next night, nor the night after that. Finally, when the quake struck on the third day, the tentative conclusion that the toads had somehow sensed the oncoming shift in the Earth's tectonic plates was drawn. This led to suggestions that their behavior could be monitored more closely to prepare for future tremors.

Quite how the toads are believed to be able to foretell the approach of an earthquake (not least several days before it) is unclear. It could be that the build-up to the quake sparks minute changes in the Earth's magnetic field. Toads are naturally attuned to the magnetic field as they utilize it when migrating back to their spawning grounds each spring. Subterranean movements might also have altered the depth, temperature, or even chemical composition of the water in the mating pool, quietly setting alarm bells ringing for the toads about how safe the pool may be for rearing their young.

Either way, it seems very small changes in the environmental chemistry of the site - small enough only to be sensed by creatures the size of the toads - were somehow able to be picked up on, causing the animals to change their behavior. Whether this ability can be harnessed to protect other towns from such similarly devastating quakes in the future remains to be seen.

Did You Know?

Seven Famous People Who Were
Meant To Travel On The Titanic

○ **GUGLIELMO MARCONI**

Nobel Prize winner and radio and telegraphy pioneer Guglielmo Marconi had been offered free passage to travel to America from Europe on board the *Titanic*. A last-minute change of schedule forced him to travel a few days earlier on board the *Lusitania*.

○ **MILTON SNAVELY HERSHEY**

You might not recognize his full name, but you'll certainly know his surname. Amazingly, another famous figure who almost became embroiled in the sinking of the *Titanic* was the inventor of Hershey's chocolate, Milton Snavely Hershey. Archivists working on the Hershey estate have unearthed a receipt for a $300 cheque - signed by Hershey and paid to the White Star line in the April of 1912. This is believed to have been a 10% down payment to reserve a stateroom on the *Titanic*'s maiden voyage. Fortunately, business intervened and both Hershey and his wife returned to America several days before the *Titanic* set sail.

○ JP MORGAN

US financier and banker John Pierpont Morgan had his own designated stateroom on board the *Titanic*, complete with its own private balcony. He, too, had been due to sail on the ship's maiden voyage, but he would have needed to cut short his spring vacation in the French resort of Aix-en-Provence. Luckily for him, Morgan decided the thrill of the maiden voyage could not compare to the quietude of the French countryside, and he remained in Provence to finish his holiday.

○ EDGAR SELWYN

One of the co-founders of MGM Studios, the actor, producer, director, and Broadway impresario Edgar Selwyn had been due to travel home from England to New York on the *Titanic*. He delayed the trip when offered the chance to proofread an early draft of a friend's debut novel in London. The friend did not intend to deliver the manuscript until April 19, forcing Selwyn to cancel his booked return journey on April 10 on board the *Titanic*.

○ THEODORE DREISER

The American novelist Theodore Dreiser was holidaying in Europe when he happened to mention to his publisher in England that he was thinking of returning home on the

Titanic. Like all good fiscally-minded publishers, Dreiser's advised him that a ticket on board another ship would be considerably cheaper. He was on board the ocean liner *Kroonland*, itself midway across the Atlantic when news of the *Titanic*'s sinking first broke.

○ BARON MORITZ VON BETHMANN

A member of the famous Bethmann family of bankers and financiers, Baron Moritz von Bethmann was in the middle of a trip around the world with friends when news of the *Titanic* disaster broke. A few days later, having arrived in Chicago, Bethmann told reporters that he and his companions had considered booking cabins on board the *Titanic*, but would have had to have cut short their trip to catch the ship at either Southampton or Cherbourg, which would have proved difficult. Undecided what the next step on their journey should be, the group had tossed a coin - and buying tickets on the *Titanic* lost out to remaining in Europe a day or two longer.

○ ROBERT BACON

A former US Secretary of State, who had served under both President Roosevelt and President Taft, Robert Bacon was the US ambassador to France in the years leading up to the sinking of the *Titanic*. Having been offered the opportunity to become a fellow at Harvard University, Bacon stepped down from his position in France in April 1912. He planned to return home to

America in style onboard the *Titanic*. As luck would have it, Bacon's replacement as ambassador, Myron T Herrick, was delayed in arriving in France, so Bacon was forced to remain in his post a few days longer than anticipated. Consequently, he and his family missed their chance to sail on the *Titanic*.

Medal Pulling

The early days of the Olympic Games were a considerably different affair from the Games we would recognize today. For one thing, the number of competing nations and athletes was only small at first: just 14 countries were involved in the 1896 Games in Athens. Of those, ten were successful in making it onto the winners' podium, with the United States finishing top of the medal table. Those 14 nations also sent a grand total of just 243 competitors (of whom almost two-thirds were local Greeks); by comparison, the 2020-21 Games in Tokyo were attended by more than 11,000 athletes, from a grand total of 206 world nations.

Not only were the participation stats different at the first modern Olympics, but so too were the sports. The 1896 Games had just nine different disciplines - athletics, cycling, fencing, gymnastics, shooting, swimming, tennis, weightlifting, and wrestling. But it did not take long for that number to begin growing as interest in the modern Olympic project grew after the turn of the century. By the 1900 Paris Games four years later, for instance, there were 95 different medal-winning events, spread across 19 separate disciplines. And among them was surely one of the most bizarre and surprising Olympic events in the organization's history.

From 1900 until 1920, bizarrely, the Olympic roster included a tug-of-war competition. The rules for this early test of brute strength were somewhat different from the other Olympic disciplines in that countries did not enter national teams, but rather individual "clubs." Competing nations were therefore permitted to enter more than one club, allowing the same nation to pick up multiple medals of different standings in the same year. At the 1904 Games in St Louis, Missouri, for instance, home clubs from the United States took all three gold, silver, and bronze medals, while at the 1908 London Games, the winners' podium was entirely British.

In the early days of the Olympics, mixed male teams were also permitted to enter events under a conglomerate Olympic flag: the gold medal for tug-of-war at the 1900 Paris games, for instance, was won by a team of six athletes comprised of three Danes and three Swedes.

The rules of the tug-of-war competition were simple. Teams had five minutes within which to pull their opponents a total of six feet, across a dividing line, in order to win. If the teams were squarely matched and after five minutes no winner could be declared, the team which had pulled the greatest total distance overall was declared the winner instead.

The rules also stipulated that no team should be allowed to wear any clothing or equipment that would give them an unfair advantage. This proved a sore point in 1908 when it was reported that a British team from Liverpool arrived at the competition all wearing "enormous shoes," that were "so heavy...it was with great effort they could lift their feet from the ground." Sensing foul play, their opposing American tug-of-war team appealed to the judges, but perhaps due to the Liverpool team being on home turf in England, their objections were ignored. In protest, the American team withdrew, and the Liverpudlians were declared the winners by default.

The Mystery Of Rudolf Diesel

Of all the people to have given their names to inventions, Rudolf Diesel's impact on not just our language but the world itself is perhaps the most remarkable.

The eponymous inventor of the diesel engine was born in Paris to a German family in 1858. Having always excelled in science and mathematics, as a young boy Rudolf was sent alone, back to his family's native Germany, to study physics under his uncle, who was a college professor. From there, Diesel continued his studies and eventually established his own workshop in which he developed more efficient fuel systems and engine dynamics. These would make him a household name and one of the most important figures of the 20th century.

As famous as Diesel's name may be - and as remarkable his impact on our world has undoubtedly become - few people know the eerie circumstances that surround his untimely and mysterious death.

By the tail-end of the 19th century, Diesel was one of the world's most celebrated engineers and industry magnates. However, his renown was not matched by any real business sense, or any longstanding financial success. By the early 1900s, his business naivety was beginning to tell. Diesel lost hundreds of thousands of marks in failed real estate investments, mothballed oil enterprises, and costly legal challenges to his numerous patents from his growing number of competitors.

The stress of it all soon began to affect his health (which had scarcely recovered from an earlier explosion at his laboratory). He was eventually advised to retreat to an isolated sanatorium in the Swiss Alps to recuperate. Despite his doctors' best efforts, Diesel's health - along with his finances - continued to decline.

Then, in 1913, Diesel received an invitation to attend the opening of a new Diesel engine factory in the UK. Having traveled from his family's home in Munich to Belgium, he boarded a small steamer ship on September 29, which was set to cross the English Channel from Antwerp to Harwich on the southeast coast of England. That evening, after taking dinner with his fellow passengers and then a brief walk around the deck for some fresh air, Diesel apparently retired to his cabin. He was never seen alive again.

The following morning, his cabin was found empty. His watch had been left by his bedside, and his nightshirt had been neatly laid out on the bed (which had not been slept in). Stranger still, Diesel's diary, which lay open on the desk, had nothing more than a solitary cross written in it for that day. A search of the ship was quickly ordered, and Diesel's hat and coat were found neatly folded below a railing at the back of the ship. Ten days later, his body was found floating in North Sea waters off the coast of the Netherlands.

When news of Diesel's death broke, rumors of foul play immediately began to swirl. Less than a year before the outbreak of the First World War, tensions across Europe were high, and against this pre-war backdrop, two competing theories soon emerged. One claimed that Diesel had been killed by British agents, who were understandably keen to prevent his ever-improving engine technology from being used by the growing and ever-improving German military. Another oppositely claimed that he had been killed by German agents, to prevent him from turning his patents over to the British government in support of the Allied cause. (Adding fuel to the fire was the later discovery that Diesel had indeed secretly arranged a meeting with the British Navy as part of his trip to England.)

Other theories claimed one of Diesel's competitors had arranged his death, and someone with vested interests on board the ferry had been charged with not only disposing of his body overboard but staging his room and his diary to make his death look like a suicide.

The truth of Diesel's mysterious death will undoubtedly never fully be known. Yet amid all the accusations of foul play, it seems likely that his history of melancholy and mental upset - as well as his worsening health and financial prospects - all eventually proved too much. And when even the restorative trip to the Swiss medical resort failed to alleviate his troubles, Diesel finally and tragically took matters into his own hands.

Island Life

From finding your way around an unfamiliar city to checking the traffic on your nightly drive home, Google Maps has undoubtedly transformed the way we travel and commute. But another, rather less expected, benefit of the technology was discovered quite by chance in 2012 when an extraordinary geographical feature was spotted. It would undoubtedly have remained entirely unknown without the aid of Google Earth's groundbreaking Landsat photographs.

It was in 2012 that an image was uploaded to Google Maps' satellite record of the Earth's surface that showed something quite remarkable in the frozen far north of Canada. Among the many hundreds of islands in the Canadian Arctic is Victoria Island - the eighth largest island in the world - which lies separated from the Canadian mainland by the often entirely icebound Coronation Gulf. Around 70 miles or so from Victoria Island's southern Coronation coastline lie a neat series of elongated glacial finger-lakes - inside one is another considerably smaller island. Continue zooming on Google's satellite picture of the area, and you'll see that in the center of *that* smaller island is another even smaller lake - and, if you keep on zooming, you'll eventually find that in that middle of *that* tiny lake is an even more minuscule island, scarcely 350 yards long!

Located at precisely 69.79° N and 108.24° W, this tiny unnamed and uninhabited island, though small, is now officially recognized as the world's largest island in a lake in an island in a lake on an island. In other words, it is the world's largest sub-sub-sub-island - an impossibly rare geographical occurrence, of which only a handful have ever been identified, let alone named or explored.

For many years, the title of the world's largest sub-sub-sub-island was held by a tiny islet nestled inside the flooded crater lake of a volcano on the aptly named Volcano Island in the Philippines - which itself lies inside another lake, Lake Taal, in the southern part of the largest and northernmost of the main Philippine islands, Luzon. When the data from Google's Landsat image of Victoria Island was analyzed, however, the tiny Arctic sub-sub-sub-island took the crown instead.

When news of the discovery was announced, geographers were quick to explain that the Canadian north is so sparsely populated, and so seldom explored, that it's likely no one had ever set foot on this newly record-breaking sub-sub-sub-island - if, for that matter, anyone had ever even *seen* it. Although the island itself is uninhabited, Victoria Island has a resident population of around 2,000 people (despite being roughly the same size as Idaho). Yet the chances of any of them ever knowing of this island's existence, nor of its geographical interest, was slim. As a result, its discovery can almost entirely be credited to the Google Maps and Google Earth projects.

Whether any larger sub-sub-sub-island in the high Arctic - or anywhere else equally unexplored, for that matter - is still awaiting discovery somewhere – well this remains to be seen.

A Wealth Of History

If someone were to ask you who the richest person in history was, who would you say?

These days, you might pick some technological giant, like Jeff Bezos, Elon Musk, or Bill Gates. If you're a history buff, you might know that inflation affects stats like these, and wisely pick someone from the past whose wealth would be comparatively even bigger today - like Andrew Carnegie, Henry Ford, or John D Rockefeller.

It's certainly true that at one point in the early 1900s, Rockefeller controlled some 90% of America's oil, and in modern terms is said to have amassed personal wealth in the region of one-third of a trillion dollars. But if we're counting people from history, we can head even further back than that.

Mansa Musa was a 14th-century emperor of Mali. Today, Mali is a landlocked desert nation in central west Africa, but at the time of Musa's reign, his empire stretched all the way from the desert city of Timbuktu to the Atlantic African coast, at modern-day Senegal. Rainforests, mountains, deserts, and vast tracts of savannah all fell under his power, and as a result, his empire grew rich in the production of a variety of products like timber, salt, copper, and even cowrie seashells (which were widely used as a form of currency). But of all the riches of his empire, however, Musa's kingdom was best known for one commodity above all others: gold.

The production of gold in Mali at that time has been estimated to have amounted to roughly one ton per year. That might not seem like a lot in modern terms, but in the ancient world, it was a figure nearly impossible to imagine. Musa's kingdom also had the benefit of lying at something of a geographical crossroads, between several rival empires and kingdoms, many of whom were often required to cross through Mali and use the desert roads and tracks over which Musa had control in order to conduct trade. As a result, even more gold flowed into his empire from outside its borders.

Moreover, the Malian Empire had a rule that any solid gold - like nuggets and ingots—could not be traded without the king being notified. Solid gold would by law become the immediate property of the crown and Musa's treasury, and would often be weighed, valued, and swapped for its equivalent in pouches of gold dust. These were used as makeshift currencies in western Africa at that time. That allowed the traders to still operate within Mali's borders, and for the king to retain all the largest and most impressive gold items for himself.

All of this made Musa an immensely rich man, and tales and anecdotes of his gargantuan wealth abound in ancient history. His army contained more men - equipped with more weaponry - than any other equivalent kingdom. And while on a pilgrimage to Mecca in the early 1300s, merely Musa's passing presence through Egypt, while en-route to Arabia, caused the country's currency to crash.

In fact, Musa's wealth was so great that some historians have estimated it to be incalculable. The reason we have no actual record of how much Musa actually possessed is that it was impossible to put it into numbers at the time. Instead, in place of facts and figures, his royal documents simply show the king holding a huge lump of gold, while clad in gold, wearing a golden crown, and sitting atop a golden throne. Images like these, these historians suggest, are intended to take the place of words and digits. His wealth was so great that it was simply impossible to quantify it or express it in sufficient terms. And if you're so wealthy we can't even describe how wealthy you are, then you're probably - and rightfully - the richest person ever to have lived.

Cold Case

In the autumn of 1991, two hikers walking through the glaciers of the Swiss Alps spotted something truly unusual.

Initially, they thought it was just trash left by other walkers, lying half-frozen atop a rock, in a deep glacial gulch filled with meltwater. But as they waded closer to retrieve it, they saw that it wasn't trash at all but a human torso.

This wasn't the scene of some terrible climbing accident or a grisly murder, however. It instantly became clear that the body had been there for very, very long time. Its skin - preserved by the ice and freezing conditions of the Alps - was now leathery and tanned brown. Beside it was a small pouch of coiled birch bark, tied up with rotten laces, and a peculiar-looking copper hand-axe, with a yew-wood and leather-bound handle. These were clearly not the modern trappings of a mountaineer, but something far more ancient.

After the body was removed, "Ötzi," as he became known (after the Ötzal mountain range where he had been found) was taken for medical and archaeological examination. His remains were carbon-dated, and the hikers' hunch that this was no modern accident soon proved correct. Incredibly, Ötzi was more than 5,000 years old and had lived in the

Alpine region of central Europe sometime in the 4th millennium BCE.

Further DNA analysis of his remains connected him genetically to a population of Neolithic farmers and earth workers (a.k.a. mound builders). Historians believe they migrated across Europe from Anatolia (in modern-day Turkey) toward the end of the Stone Age, around 8,000–6,000 years ago. But these same medical examinations went on to make several more remarkable discoveries that soon shed light not only on Ötzi's culture and his people's history but on the increasingly questionable manner of his death.

X-rays and body scans revealed a huge wound on the back of Ötzi's skull. The remaining soft tissues of his brain also showed considerable trauma and contusion, suggesting he had suffered a terrible blow to the back of his head. There was also a large puncture wound in the middle of his hand that appeared to be defensive - as if Ötzi had attempted to grab the blade of a weapon held or pushed toward him. That wound appears to have already begun healing, however, by the time Ötzi was mortally wounded. An arrowhead was found embedded in his shoulder, deep enough to nick an artery in his neck.

He may have lived long enough to make some manner of getaway, but it seems fairly certain that this neck wound would have eventually caused Ötzi to bleed out. It was perhaps at this point that he fell into the gulch (a narrow and steep-sided ravine) - bashing his head on a rock or ice on the way down. Then maybe his body fell neatly between two large stones that prevented it from being washed away. Covered by more than 10 ft of compacted snow, his remains would have become mummified and perfectly preserved, leading to his discovery all those years later.

The historical importance of Ötzi's makeshift grave was enormous, and what historians could piece together from his discovery shed extraordinary new light on what we understood about the early Europeans. The copper used to make his axe, for instance, pushed the development of copper artifacts in Europe back more than 1,000 years than had been previously thought. But the manner and number of his injuries also allowed historians to gain a better understanding of his final hours, and most came to the same conclusion: it seemed clear that Ötzi had been murdered.

Precisely who had killed Ötzi and why was uncertain, of course, yet there were nevertheless a handful of clues. The discovery of his axe was an intriguing additional detail, as a pure copper tool like that suggested affluence at the time of Ötzi's life. Was he fleeing robbers at the time of his death, who were trying to steal his most treasured possession? Or had he stolen the axe from someone else, and was being hunted down by those attempting to get it back? Such are the circumstances, we will doubtless never know for sure the answers to questions like these - and Ötzi's mysterious death, ultimately, remains one of the most fascinating and enthralling cold cases in all ancient human history.

Did You Know?

Seven More Remarkable Preserved Humans

○ **ARDEN WOMAN**

In 1942, the body of a woman in her early twenties was found in Bredmose Bog, an area of peat marshland in Hindsted in central Denmark. Analysis of her remains suggested she had died almost 3,500 years ago, sometime around 1400 BCE. Her hair was dark blonde and tied up in two pigtails on the sides of her head, kept neatly below a style of early woolen headwear known as a sprang cap. Unlike other so-called "bog bodies" - found perfectly preserved in the cold, oxygen-poor bogs of northern Europe - Arden Woman showed no sign of violent death, and precisely what her cause of death may have been remains a total mystery.

○ **CASHEL MAN**

Cashel Man is the name given to the body of a young adult male, perhaps around 25 years of age, that was discovered on farmland near the town of Cashel in Laois, central Ireland, in 2011. His remains were found to be perhaps as much as 4,000 years old - dating from the early Bronze Age - making him one of the oldest ancient bodies ever discovered in Europe. As if that weren't remarkable enough, in a gruesome twist to Cashel Man's discovery, he was found with several broken bones (including a badly broken leg) and with a noose tied around his neck. This suggested he had died a violent death, likely by hanging or strangulation.

○ "GINGER"

The Gebelein Predynastic Mummies, as they are officially known, are a set of six naturally mummified bodies that were discovered in remote graves in the Egyptian desert by British Egyptologists at the end of the 19th century. One of the mummies was affectionately dubbed "Ginger" in light of his most extraordinary feature: his bright gingery red hair. While many of the remarkable items and artifacts discovered alongside the mummies remained in Egypt, the six bodies are now housed in the British Museum, where "Ginger" has been on permanent display since 1900.

○ ELLING WOMAN

In 1938, the poorly-preserved remains of a young Bronze Age woman were found in a bog in the Danish town of Silkeborg. The body was wrapped in two cloaks - one made of sheepskin, the other of leather - and her hair was tied up in a long and elaborate braid almost a meter long. Elling Woman, as she became known, was one of two bodies removed from the same region, both of whom were subsequently found to have been hanged. Historians and archaeologists now believe that the pair may both have been human sacrifices.

○ OLD CROGHAN MAN

Old Croghan Man is the name of an astonishingly well-preserved body, dating from sometime in the western European Iron Age, around 300 BCE, that was discovered in Ireland in 2003. His remains were so well preserved that scientists were able to take his fingerprints, and found that his nails had apparently been well cared for during his life, and showed a similar level of treatment to a modern manicure. It was suggested that the man may have been some kind of ancient chief. The man is calculated (based on his arm span) to have stood approximately between 5 ft 11.5 inches and 6 ft 6 in (1.98 m) tall, which is considered to be exceptionally tall for the period when he lived. As a chief or king, he perhaps had been sacrificed by his people when a harvest failed under his rule (for which he would be held spiritually responsible) or else to ensure a better harvest the following year (as the death of such a high-status individual would be considered a prime gift to the gods).

○ HARALDSKÆR WOMAN

In 1835, the ancient remains of a woman in her fifties, dubbed Haraldskær Woman, were found in a bog in

Denmark. At the time, it was widely presumed that the woman was Queen Gunnhild of Norway, who lived and ruled in northern Europe around 1000 CE, but modern technology has since predated her remains and found her to be even older: Haraldskær Woman lived sometime during Europe's pre-Roman Iron Age, around 490 BCE - some 2,500 years ago.

○ **UNNAMED PRE-INCAN**

In 2021, the astonishingly well-preserved mummified body of a mummified adult, perhaps in their mid-20s, was found in a grave on the coast of Peru. The body was found in a crouched position - with its limbs tied together and its hands tied at the wrist and held in front of its face. It was wrapped in cloth, which was how many ancient Peruvian people were prepared after death in the culture's funeral practices. Although archaeologists in Peru are still figuring out the true age, identity, and importance of the person's death, it is hoped that their discovery will shed light on the history of the peoples who lived along the Pacific coast of South America before the rise of the Incan Empire more than 1,500 years ago.

Everybody Dance Now

When you think of a plague, your first thought is probably of the bubonic Black Death that swept across medieval Europe and Asia - spurred on by huge numbers of infected rats and mice - for more than three centuries. But midway through all of that, the French city of Strasbourg was afflicted by another much less familiar and much more unusual plague. Though one that, it seems, proved just as easy to catch.

It was one morning in the July of 1518 that a local woman identified only as Frau Troffea stepped out of her house in Strasbourg and began inexplicably dancing in the street. No doubt much to the concern of her neighbors, it soon became clear that Frau Troffea was not able to stop. She eventually collapsed from exhaustion in the midsummer heat. She was helped back inside her home and took to her bed for a few days to recover - but once she was back on her feet, she headed back outside, and resumed her wild dancing as if nothing had happened.

Incredibly, this cycle continued for several days, whereupon it soon began to afflict other people too. Within a week, Frau Troffea had been joined by 30 more local Strasbourgeans. All of them began wildly and unstoppably dancing, even if they fell to the ground injured, exhausted, or worse. Unsure of how to stop this bizarre "dancing plague," the local authorities thought it best to find the dancers somewhere safe in which to do it. The local guildhall was cleared, and the dancers ushered into it, with live music put on to give the frenzied hoofers something to dance along to.

The hope was that when the music stopped the dancers would simply cease too, but instead, the opposite happened. Not only did the dancers keep dancing, but with a music-filled dancehall now open for business, more and more people began to join in. For weeks, the nonstop dancing contagion rumbled on in the city, until by September more than 400 people had been afflicted. Some of those involved even danced so long and so hard that they collapsed and died from the sheer exertion of it all.

Eventually, after more than two months, the craze finally began to abate and had all but ended by the late autumn. At the time, explanations for this inexplicable and unstoppable dance party ranged from disorders of the temperature of the blood to possession by demonic spirits. Today, it's been more rationally suggested a rare form of food poisoning known as ergot, caused by contaminated rye flour, may have caused fierce convulsions that could have seemed like wild dance moves to those unfamiliar with its effects. Whatever the true cause of the "dancing plague" may have been, however, it is undoubtedly among the most curious tales in Europe's long history.

Evidentially!

English is often claimed to have more words than any other language. Estimates of just how many words we have range from around 250,000 to well over a million (depending, that is, on precisely what you consider to be a word a to be!)

That enormous vocabulary can make English a surprisingly difficult language to master. Although our grammar is relatively straightforward, the sheer number of words we have at our disposal makes learning, remembering, using, and understanding all of them quite a considerable challenge for any outside learner. But when it comes to the difficulties of learning a new language, English has nothing on an astonishing Melanesian language known as Fasu.

Fasu (or Namo Me, as it is also known) is a language in the East Kutubuan family, spoken in a small central region of Papua New Guinea. Linguists working in the area are still cataloging and describing the language today. One of the most remarkable features their work has uncovered so far is a complex six-tier grammatical system known as evidentiality.

In linguistics, evidentiality is a grammatical phenomenon in which a speaker is required by the rules of their language to explain how they know what it is they're saying. Think of it this way: in English, we have to add an 's' to the end of a word when we're talking about more than one of them. Speakers of Fasu are likewise compelled by the grammar of their language to change and inflect what they say to show the person they're talking to how they came to know it.

So a speaker making casual conversation, for instance, would have to alter a simple statement like *It's raining* depending on whether they know it to be raining because of direct participation (it rained on them); visual sensory participation (they can see that it is raining); nonvisual sensory participation (they can hear it raining, for instance); inferential information (they have spotted people's clothes are wet, and so can infer that it is raining); reported information (they have spoken to someone who had been out in the rain); or if they heard from another known source (they saw a weather report on television, for instance).

In English, of course, we would have to add extra information like this into the sentence itself, coming out with something along the lines of *Mike says it's raining outside!* or *It's raining - I can hear it on the roof of the house.* But in Fasu, the verb form for the word *rain* itself would be inflected to show on what type of knowledge or evidence the speaker was basing their statement.

Incredibly, this kind of *here's-how-I-know-what-I'm-talking-about* grammatical system is actually relatively common around the word. You'll find similar systems in many native North American languages, as well as in many of the languages of West Africa and the Amazon basin. What makes Fasu so astonishing, however, is how complex a system of evidentiality it has. Few languages on Earth have established anything near a six-part system of evidence reporting - surely making Fasu one of the most challenging languages for anyone wishing to learn it!

Shower Power

Alfred Hitchcock's *Psycho* is one of cinema's greatest-ever horror movies. The tale of a quiet young man who lives in an isolated motel with his mother - as well as the gruesome, mysterious murders that take place there - has remained enduring popular (and endlessly terrifying!) since its release back in 1960.

Compared to some horror movies today, of course, the onscreen violence in *Psycho* might seem relatively tame. But back in the 1960s, movie audiences weren't quite so accustomed to seeing brutal murders and bloody violence on the big screen as we are today. In fact, proving just how tame and censorious cinema still was in the early sixties, *Psycho* was the first film in movie history to break the bathroom taboo, and show a toilet being flushed on the big screen!

As a result, movie audiences were utterly terrified by what Hitchcock had put together - most notably, the now-famous shower scene, in which the film's heroine, Marion Crane (played by Janet Leigh) encounters the murderer at the Bates Motel for the first (and last!) time.

The shower scene in *Psycho* barely lasts three minutes in total, but filming it - in the careful detail Hitchcock characteristically demanded - took a full six days of shooting. It was originally delayed because Leigh caught a cold (and so, understandably, did not want to spend all day soaking wet). Filming eventually got underway on December 17, 1959. It has been estimated that a total of 78 individual shots, including several extreme close-ups, were required for the sequence, which Hitchcock claimed was shot from more than 60 different camera angles. The longest of these individual shots was just 45 seconds - with all the individual footage spliced together in the editing process using 52 individual cuts.

Not only was the sheer number of camera shots and setups so complex, but many of the individual shots Hitchcock wanted to include proved logistically difficult. They also required unique solutions to achieve on-screen. Among them, Hitchcock wanted an upward shot of the water falling from the showerhead, directly toward the camera - which required the construction of a specially elongated lens, so that the water would not obscure the shot. The innermost holes of the showerhead were then blocked with putty, and the camera was placed in such a position that it remained dry while the water sprayed down around it.

Another problem emerged when it came to showing the blood from the shower scene trickling down the drain. The fake stage blood that would ordinarily have been used in a scene like this soon proved too thin when mixed with the water in the bathtub. It looked unrealistic on film. Several alternatives were suggested and concocted, and Hitchcock's stagehands tried a host of different mixtures in an attempt to make the fake blood behave more realistically. In the end, the stage blood had to be removed altogether, and a somewhat unusual replacement was brought in instead. Knowing that the movie was to be filmed in black and white (and so any suitably viscous substance would do, regardless of its color), Hitchcock settled on Hershey's chocolate syrup. The blood seen spiraling down the plug hole in Marion's shower, ultimately, was actually an ice cream sauce you could pick up at any grocery store!

The Story's End

After the success of the original 1995 *Toy Story* movie, the producers at Walt Disney Studios quickly commissioned a sequel.

Originally, they intended the follow-up to be a short-form, straight-to-DVD movie. They hoped it would match the straight-to-VHS success of *The Return of Jafar*, the sequel to their smash hit *Aladdin*, which made $100 million in videotape sales alone. However, the producers soon realized that the sequel was a much stronger idea than they had initially anticipated. Seeing even more dollar signs on the horizon, they requested the production team add a further 12 minutes to its run time - qualifying it for a full theatrical release in cinemas around the world—and began to prep for a full-blown follow-up movie. A release date was scheduled, a promotional budget was put together, and the team was given a year or two to pull the entire film together.

In the early days of computer-generated animation, adding 12 minutes of footage to a project that was already underway was easier said than done. Still, the *Toy Story 2* team soon set about fleshing out the script, drawing up storyboards for the new scenes and entering the additional coded material into the film's CGI program. All was going swimmingly until one of the production team (who has hitherto remained anonymous...) entered an incorrect computer command - '/bin/rm-r-f*' into the master computer, on which all the movie's code to date was stored. The error was not caught in time, and as the code began to cycle through the system, *Toy Story 2* began to be slowly and irreversibly deleted!

In an interview after the movie came out, Pixar Studios co-founder Ed Catmull recalled that the cowboy hat worn by the movie's main character, Woody, suddenly disappeared from on screen as they were working on it. Next, his boots vanished. Then, after a moment, Woody himself disappeared. As the erroneous line of code began filtering through the computer system, entire sequences of the movie started to be deleted from the master drive. By the time the mistake was spotted, and the plug was pulled - thereby stopping the deletion in its tracks - around 90% of the movie was gone.

In desperation, the team ran to the computer's backup system, only to find that entirely by fateful coincidence, the automatic backup system had failed. It seemed the movie was back to square one. Catmull estimated that it would take the entire team a year just to get back to where they were before the code breach; unfortunately for them, the movie's theatrical release date was now one year away.

In a plot twist worthy of a Pixar movie itself, however, the team suddenly remembered that one of the movie's technical directors, Galyn Susman, was currently working at home on maternity leave. Once a week during her convalescence, Susman took an entire copy of the movie as it was to date to work on at home. That meant the entire $100 million production was now housed in a single computer on the other side of Los Angeles. Having sped across the city, Jacobs and Susman loaded the machine into the passenger seat of his car, swaddled it in blankets, and then drove back to the studio slowly at 35mph to ensure it arrived in one piece.

Happily, although some of that week's footage had indeed been irreversibly deleted, Susman had enough of the movie on her backup for the team to largely pick up where they had left off. The remainder of the production passed by without a hitch. The team was amply rewarded for their efforts, too. When the movie was finally released to cinemas in 1999, it almost doubled the box office gross of the previous film - taking more than half a billion dollars - and was nominated for a slew of prizes at the following year's awards season.

Smoot By Smoot

Say you had to measure the length of a wall or a road, for instance. Chances are you would grab your tape measure and count it out in feet, yards, or meters. But at the Massachusetts Institute of Technology in the mid-1950s, an entirely different unit of measurement was used that has since become something of a local standard.

Oliver R Smoot was a Lambda Chi Alpha fraternity pledge at MIT in October 1958. As part of his initiation to the Lambda Chi house, a challenge was concocted by the house pledge master in which that year's pledges were made to measure the entire length of the Harvard Bridge - connecting the cities of Boston and Cambridge - using Smoot as their only measuring apparatus. (Smoot was reportedly chosen not just because, at 5 ft, 7 inches tall, he was the shortest of the Lambda Chi pledges, but because his unusual surname sounded the most like an actual unit of measurement!)

The pledges headed out of the campus to the bridge, whereupon Smoot soon set about repeatedly lying down - head to toe, from one end of the bridge to the other - while his fellow Lambda Chis ensured their measurements were as accurate as possible. After several hours, it was at long last determined that the bridge was just over 364.4 "smoots" in length, and therefore given Smoot's height, it must be 2,035 ft long. Remarkably, given how makeshift their measuring technique was, the Lambda Chis' calculations were not far wrong: the bridge is in fact just under 2,165 feet long (or rather $387\frac{3}{4}$ smoots).

Back on the campus, the prank soon caught the imagination of the rest of the MIT students, and it wasn't long before the joke - and the "smoot" as a makeshift unit of measurement - were being reported in the college newspaper, and the local press. Soon, a local campaign had been launched to have the bridge permanently divided into Smoot-based milestones.

Today, these painted markers remain in use. Each smoot is marked onto the sidewalk of the Harvard Bridge, with a digit written out every 10 smoots to allow them to be more easily counted. When the bridge was renovated in the 1980s, the smoots were repainted and restored, and today are repainted each semester by a new Lambda Chi pledge. At long last, a plaque honoring Smoot's bizarre contribution to local lore was unveiled on the bridge as part of a 50th-anniversary event in 2008.

Did You Know?

Seven More Forgotten Measurements

○ **BARLEYCORN**

These days, you're unlikely to come across barleycorn other than in a grainfield, but in terms of measurement, a barleycorn is a name given to one-third of an inch. Although it's seldom been used since the 16th and 17th centuries, there is at least one place in which you may still see barleycorns in use today. The number system on which shoe sizes are based is still measured in barleycorns.

○ **BUTTON**

While a foot is one-third of a yard, and one-twelfth of a foot is an inch, if one-third of an inch is a barleycorn, then one-twelfth of an inch is called a button.

○ **OXGANG**

Also known as a bovate, in ancient England and parts of Europe an oxgang was a unit used to measure area - in particular, the area of fields, pastureland, and farmland. The word itself hints at how large the unit was, and where it originally came from: an oxgang is literally an 'ox-going' and is based on the amount of land a single ox could be expected to plow in 12 months (approximately 15 acres). As such, it was equal to one-eighth of a larger unit, called a carucate, which was based on the amount of land a team of eight oxen could work in an entire year.

○ HOBBIT

Here's a word you'll no doubt know, but a meaning you likely won't! Long before JRR Tolkien created the world of Middle Earth, a hobbit, or hobbet, was a unit of volume in use in medieval Wales, equal to around two and a half bushels (20 dry gallons today). Differences between the sale of wet and dry goods - as well as issues caused by converting Welsh measurements into English measurements - eventually proved the hobbit's downfall. It was replaced by the more standardized Winchester system of volume that remained in use in England until the early 1800s (and still forms the basis of the American system of weights and measures to this day).

○ SHIPLOAD

It sounds almost too general a term to ever be of any use, but at the height of the UK's coal trade in the 19th and early 20th centuries, a shipload was a precise unit of measurement equal to the standard load of a collier ship. In technical terms, a shipload of coal is equal to 949,760 lbs. One shipload was also equal to one-twentieth of a unit known as a keel, which was the standard load of a single coal-carrying keelboat in Newcastle-upon-Tyne, one of the biggest coal-producing cities in England.

○ DONKEYPOWER

It was the Scottish engineer James Watt who first introduced the world to the horsepower unit way back in the late 18th century. Watt observed that a horse was able to lift a weight of 180 lbs., attached to a 75-ft-circumference millwheel so that the wheel rotated 144 times in one hour. That meant the wheel traveled 181 ft every minute - based on which Watt calculated the horse's 'power' to be roughly 33,000 foot-pounds-per-minute. But what if you need to describe the power of a machine less powerful than a horse? For that, you need a donkey power - a unit of work equal to one-third that of a single horsepower. It was proposed in the late 1800s to give engineers a workable unit with which to compare the power of smaller machines than the engines studied by Watt.

○ CANDLEPOWER

Candlepower is a now obsolete unit of luminosity, roughly equal to the light emitted by a single candle. Although different candles understandably have different strengths, in modern terms the candlepower unit was defined as roughly equal to 0.9 candela - the unit now used in the official SI system to measure luminous intensity.

Catastrophe!

Over the long centuries since the foundation of the Catholic Church, there have been quite a few tales of bizarre eccentrics and scandalous oddballs rising to the top and being proclaimed pope.

The 15th-century pope Sixtus IV, for instance, had a child with his sister (as well as five other illegitimate children) and made six of his nephews into cardinals. (He also commissioned the Sistine Chapel, so his reign wasn't entirely bad...)

Way back in the mid-11th century, Pope Benedict IX attained the papacy in 1032 when he was just 12 years old. Although not much is known about what his papal rule actually entailed, the decision to effectively place a child in charge of the church does not seem to have gone down well. One later historian dismissed Benedict as little more than "a demon from hell."

Of all the popes in the history books, however, two names are often highlighted for the bizarre acts they carried out during their reign. One, Pope Stephen VI, we'll meet a little later here - while the other, Pope Gregory IX, is popularly said to have used his powers to effectively declare war on Europe's cats.

Gregory became pope in the spring of 1227 and ruled until his death at the age of 70 (although some reports claim he was in fact well in his late nineties) in 1241. It was six years into his papacy, in 1231, that he issued an infamous papal bull (a public order) known as the *Vox in Rama*. In it, he denounced a heretical sect, known as the Luciferianists, who had recently grown in power and popularity in Germany.

As part of their initiation into the sect, the pope explained in his bull, Luciferianist members are supposedly approached by a gigantic dog-sized toad, who speaks to them and invites them to join the group. If they accept, a weak-looking man magically appears, and when they kiss his hands, all memory of their Catholic faith is wiped from their minds. They then sit down to enjoy a vast and perpetually replenishing banquet, and eat until they can eat no more. Then a statue of a black cat comes to life, the members take turns to kiss its backside and are ultimately initiated into the sect.

Given the wildness of that account, the reports on which Gregory had based his proclamation were likely somewhat exaggerated, it's fair to say. But his description of this bizarre ritual so affected the superstitious medieval Europeans that anything associated with it soon came to be viewed with suspicion - including their pet cats.

The story goes that Pope Gregory's *Vox in Rama* proclamation turned many people's minds against their cats. Until then, they had been little more than household companions and a handy means of controlling vermin. Unfortunately, the people of Europe then set about slaying their cats in such enormous numbers that the population of vermin exploded - ushering in, so the story goes, the flea-ridden, plague-carrying rats that caused the Black Death.

Whether the pope's holy war on cats was indeed an instigating factor in the outbreak of Europe's plague is admittedly a little questionable. Some later historians have cast doubt on whether his words were indeed taken so literally by the medieval Europeans. The wording of his papal bull, however, and his bizarre account of that bottom-kissing ritual is all entirely true - so perhaps there is at least some truth to this extraordinary catastrophe!

Historical Accuracy

Cate Blanchett has twice played Queen Elizabeth I on screen, both times in movies directed by acclaimed Indian filmmaker Shekhar Kapur - and both times earning herself a nomination for the Academy Award for Best Actress.

Her first performance was 1999's biographical drama *Elizabeth*, which focused on the early years of Queen Elizabeth's reign, beginning with her rise to the throne in 1558 after the death of her elder half-sister, Mary I. The second was Kapur's 2007 sequel, *Elizabeth: The Golden Age*, which fictionalized the events of the later years of her rule, including the famous Babington Plot to assassinate her, and culminating in England seeing off the threat of invasion posed by the Spanish Armada in 1588.

After the success of the 1999 film, there was immediate interest in Blanchett reprising her role as Elizabeth I, but scheduling conflicts and filming delays meant the project did not get off the ground until the mid-2000s. *The Golden Age* was a more ambitious project from the outset, with a budget almost twice that of the first film. The majority of the film was made at the world-famous Shepperton Studios in Surrey, England. However, the film's lavish production design budget meant many real-life locations across the UK could be used in place of palaces and buildings that Elizabeth would have known and used during her reign.

Eilean Donan Castle, in the Kyle of Lochalsh in Scotland, for instance, was used in place of Fotheringay Castle, where Elizabeth's first cousin once removed, Mary, Queen of Scots, was imprisoned and eventually executed. Ely Cathedral in Cambridgeshire was used in place of one of the chambers in Whitehall, London, where Elizabeth meets with the Spanish ambassador in an attempt to see off the threat of the armada diplomatically. And the Catholic Cathedral of Westminster, in Victoria in central London, was used for a series of scenes set in the court of Elizabeth's Spanish rival, King Philip II.

When it came to filming scenes set in and around London's famous St. Paul's Cathedral, however, the filmmakers were faced with a problem.

The St. Paul's Cathedral we know today - with its famous domed roof, designed by the acclaimed architect Sir Christopher Wren - was built in the late 17th century, long after Elizabeth died in 1603. The cathedral of St. Paul's that she would have known was an entirely different wooden-framed building, known as Old St Paul's. It was one of the many buildings destroyed by the Great Fire of London in 1666.

The construction of Old St Paul's was begun under the Norman kings of England in the 11th century, with the

114

building then greatly expanded under Elizabeth's ancestors during the 1200s and 1300s. But in the early years of Elizabeth's reign, in 1561, the grand central steeple of the Norman church was struck by lightning and all but destroyed. The economic situation in England at the time meant that the spire could not be repaired right away, and the cathedral remained in a state of disrepair for several decades.

The makers of *The Golden Age* ultimately needed to find a suitable real-life English cathedral that not only resembled a building that was no longer standing but was built in an entirely different Norman Gothic style. Moreover, it had to be easily made to look damaged and in need of repair on the screen. Incredibly, they found it!

As luck would have it, Winchester Cathedral - one of the largest in the UK, if not all of Europe - resembled the Norman Gothic style of London's Old St Paul's. Plus, at the time of filming, it was undergoing considerable regeneration and renovation. As a result, the filmmakers could incorporate the genuine renovations at Winchester into the plot of *The Golden Age*, making its repairs look as if St Paul's was being repaired following the lightning strike. The masonry and equipment the renovators at Winchester were using were already historically accurate, as the renovation team was keen to match the style of the original stonework at Winchester as closely as possible. So, all they had to do was don appropriate Elizabethan-era clothing and get ready for their closeups!

Ghost Town

In 1920, an edition of a bimonthly magazine called the *White Pine Series of Architectural Monographs* was published. In it, Massachusetts architect Hubert G Ripley introduced a series of photographs of a delightfully quaint New England village named Stotham.

Painting a picture of a quiet, genteel settlement away from the hustle and bustle of nearby towns and cities, Ripley introduced his piece with these famous lines from the English poet Thomas Gray's *Elegy Written in a Country Churchyard*:

> *Far from the madding crowd's ignoble strife,*
> *Their sober wishes never learn'd to stray;*
> *Along the cool sequester'd vale of life,*
> *They kept the noiseless tenor of their way.*

The town, he went on to explain, had been founded back in the late 17th century by a young Puritan couple named Zabdiel Podbury and Drusilla Ives. They had abandoned their home in the town of Stoke-on-Tritham in England in the spring of 1689 and set sail for Massachusetts Bay aboard an English bark called the *Promise*. Once in the New World, the couple named their new home after their home back in

England. Over time, "Stoke" and "Tritham" slowly merged into one, and the new name of Stotham was born in its place.

Over the centuries, Ripley recounted, the town had grown as ever more quaint wooden buildings were added to it. Eventually, it came "in later days...to be regarded as a typical example - although perhaps not so well known - of the unspoiled New England Village." The photographs Ripley included alongside more than proved that point, showing a picturesque village, peopled by smartly-dressed men and women, standing proudly outside their beautiful homes and cottages.

It sounds like a truly picture-perfect town, ideal for an escape to the country. There was just one small problem: Stotham does not exist.

The article Ripley had compiled was actually a hoax, and the town of Stotham - as well as its legendary founders, and even the town in England from which they were supposed to have fled - was all fake. The pictures were the only true part of the piece: they were all genuine photographs, taken of quaint homes in several towns from across New England. The images had all been edited out of previous editions of the magazine, but rather than simply discard them, Ripley concocted a fake story and used them to illustrate it. That way, the people whose homes were being photographed were not overlooked and would still have their moment in the spotlight - albeit in a not entirely truthful way!

Incredibly, Ripley's hoax tale was not discovered for more than two decades, when in the mid-1940s, researchers looking into the back catalog of the magazine at the Library of Congress were surprised to be unable to find Stotham on any local maps. When the random assortment of photographs was noticed too, the deception was at long last revealed, over 20 years after it first went to print.

Building Blocks

How tall a tower would you think you could build using kids' building blocks?

You might think that question would depend on nothing more than the number of blocks at your disposal. However, just as with real buildings and structures, the taller a tower is, the more weight is put onto its foundations. And ultimately, the more unsteady it becomes, the more structurally sound its construction needs to be.

So long as those problems are addressed, however, the sky is quite literally the limit - or at least, it was for a team of four Boy Scouts from Grenoble, in southern France, who smashed the record for building-block tower-making in 2021.

The four boys - Thibault Piollat, Jonathan Wild, Enzo Bruder-Jeannot, and Antoine Sanchez - decided to take on the challenge in the autumn of 2020. They spent the next several months working on their design, figuring out the best blocks to use, tracking down suppliers willing to provide enough blocks for the attempt, and finding a location suitable for their extraordinary plans. Eventually, the team decided to use a type of building block popular among children in France known as *Kapla* blocks - short and rather flat wooden planks that look a little like flattened versions of the blocks used to play Jenga. It did take some time to track down a toy supplier keen to provide them with the 11,000 blocks they required for their tower!

Once all the preparations had been made, the four boys finally began their attempt the following summer. On 27 June 2021, at a climbing center in the town of Mulhouse in Alsace, northeast France, they started to get to work.

All the elements of their plan worked perfectly. To give their tower strength and avoid it collapsing, they used an ingenious Y-shaped design. By building it in a climbing center, the boys could use the ropes, pulleys, and other rock-climbing equipment to easily climb to the top of it as they went. The center's immense ceiling meant that they could build to an enormous height indoors, away from the wind. Eventually, after working for more than 16 hours, they completed all 151 stories of the tower - reaching an extraordinary height of just over $61\frac{1}{2}$ ft and beating the previous record by almost 1.6 ft!

Quick Study

Many authors are known for being painstaking in their work and publish only a handful of books in their lifetime. *Games of Thrones* author George RR Martin, for instance, began working on the sixth penultimate installment in his popular series in 2010; by 2022, it was reported he still had around one-third of the book left to write. And Harper Lee is best known for her Pulitzer-winning novel, *To Kill A Mockingbird*. Its much-anticipated sequel *Go Set A Watchman* was published 55 years later in 2015 but was later revealed to have merely been an earlier draft of her first and only book.

Other writers, however, work remarkably rapidly. Kazuo Ishiguro wrote *The Remains of the Day* in just four weeks. Horror author Stephen King admits to writing at least 2,000 words every day, including weekends and holidays (and wrote the first draft of *The Running Man* in less than a week). And Robert Louis Stevenson wrote *The Strange Case of Dr Jekyll and Mr. Hyde* in just three days - then spent another three days rewriting it after he threw the first draft on the fire!

Another author known for his speed and prolificness (that is, abundant productivity) was Arthur Conan Doyle. In 1886, he not only finished his debut novel in just three weeks but in doing so created one of the most famous and enduring characters in all literary history.

At the time, Doyle was 27 years old and working as a doctor at a medical practice in the town of Southsea, Hampshire, on the south coast of England. He had always enjoyed writing alongside his medical training and his work. Despite the pressures of his practice, Doyle had already published several short stories in national magazines. This story - a novel initially called *A Tangled Skein*, written between consultations with his patients at his office - was to be his first full-length work.

Initially, the tale was rejected by several publishers, and Doyle was compelled to make some amendments and resubmit it several months later, under a revised title, *A Study in Scarlet*. It was eventually bought up by a London publisher, Ward Lock & Co., and appeared in full in the 1887 edition of *Beeton's Christmas Annual*. The following year, the story was published in book form for the first time. Yet despite being critically well received, neither it nor the Christmas annual failed to attract much public attention and was considered a financial failure.

One person who had enjoyed the book, however, was Joseph Stoddart, the editor of another London periodical, *Lippincott's Monthly Magazine*. While at a dinner party in 1889, he convinced Doyle to write a second novel featuring the same character from the first - an intriguing character by the name of Sherlock Holmes. In return, Stoddart offered to serialize the entire novel, across several editions of the magazine, to build up readers' interest across each monthly installment.

Though initially unconvinced, Doyle nevertheless set to work, and the first part of his second novel, *The Sign of Four*, was published the following year. Stoddart's plan to divide the story into cliffhanger episodes worked wonders too. His readers were soon enraptured with the intricate detective story Doyle had written - as well as its central character, Mr. Holmes.

Over the years that followed, Doyle went on to write over 50 more Sherlock Holmes novels and short stories, going on to become one of the most successful authors of his time. When he grew tired of the tales himself, he even deliberately raised the fee he demanded from his publishers, presuming they would never accept his demands and refuse to publish any more tales. To his surprise, they more than met his demands, and he was compelled to continue writing. Not bad for a character he had created in just 21 days!

Did You Know?

Seven More Facts About Sherlock Holmes

○ **SHERLOCK WAS A REAL PERSON**

...Or at least, he was *based* on a real person. In creating the world's greatest detective, Doyle was inspired by a medical lecturer he had known at university in Edinburgh, Dr Joseph Bell, who supposedly had such an instinctive and intuitive knowledge of medicine that he could diagnose patients simply by looking at them. Doyle later took his former professor's extraordinary perceptiveness and used it as the basis of Sherlock Holmes' similarly remarkable intuition.

○ **"SHERLOCK" WASN'T HIS ORIGINAL NAME**

Doyle was a cricket fan, and according to legend spotted the unusual name "Sherlock" listed among a roster of players one day while at Marylebone Cricket Club in London. Before then, his most famous character had been due to be called "Sherrinford Holmes."

○ **SHERLOCK'S ADDRESS IS (ALMOST) REAL**

Famously, Sherlock Holmes lived at 221B Baker Street in central London. If you were to write a letter to that address today, it would arrive at the official Sherlock Holmes Museum - despite the museum itself occupying premises at 239 Baker Street. Brilliantly, the British Post Office has given the museum a special dispensation allowing it to operate under a different postal address, honoring Doyle's creation.

○ OSCAR WILDE WAS A BIG FAN

Additionally, in attendance at the same dinner party where Doyle was asked to write a second Holmes story was Oscar Wilde, who happily told Doyle that he had very much enjoyed his first story. Although best known as a poet and playwright, Wilde agreed to write a novel for serialization in *Lippencott's* magazine too alongside Doyle's. The story Wilde went on to submit was his only novel, *The Picture of Dorian Grey*.

○ SHERLOCK IS THE MOST PORTRAYED CHARACTER IN HISTORY

The year 1900 saw the release of a 30-second silent short film called *Sherlock Holmes Baffled*. Though not based on any of Doyle's stories, the short is now recognized as the very first on-screen appearance of Sherlock Holmes in cinema history. He has gone on to be portrayed more than 240 times in movies and television series since and is now widely considered the most portrayed character in movie history (although Count Dracula is sometimes given the top spot instead!).

❍ DETECTIVES USE MAGNIFYING GLASSES THANKS TO HIM

...Or at least, we like to think they do! It was Doyle's stories of Sherlock Holmes whipping out his trusty magnifying glass to scan for clues that gave us our traditional idea of detectives and investigators doing just that.

❍ HE NEVER ACTUALLY SAID HIS MOST FAMOUS CATCHPHRASE

Not once in any of Doyle's stories does Sherlock Holmes utter the immortal line, "Elementary, my dear Watson!" He does exclaim "Elementary!" on several occasions, and addresses his god friend as "My dear Watson" - but never in the same sentence.

Mary Who?

The classic nursery rhyme *Mary Had a Little Lamb* first appeared in print as a poem, written by the writer Sarah Josepha Hale, in an American collection of rhymes published in 1830:

Mary had a little lamb,
Its fleece was white as snow.
And everywhere that Mary went
The lamb was sure to go.

Hale's original version of rhyme actually has three eight-line verses, with the lamb accompanying Mary to school at the end of the first; being turned out of the school by the teacher in the second; and the other schoolchildren wondering why the lamb appears so attached to Mary in the third.

Hale reportedly based the rhyme on a real event that had taken place while she was employed as a schoolteacher in New Hampshire in the early 1800s, in which a student named Mary had turned up one morning with her pet lamb beside her, and brought it into the classroom. The uninvited visitor quickly proved far too distracting for the other pupils, and Hale told Mary to leave the lamb outside for the rest of the day. Once school was over, Mary went outside and the lamb immediately ran up to her like a dog running back to its owner. The other pupils asked Hale why the lamb was behaving that way, and Hale invented the rhyme both as a moralistic teaching aid and as a way of immortalizing the event.

That version of the story, which has long been recounted by several of Hale's biographers, was for many years the most accepted version of the events that led to the rhyme's publication. That was until 1876 when a 70-year-old woman named Mary Tyler claimed that she was in fact the girl from the original poem, and that the rhyme had actually been written for her by a young student teacher named John Roulstone.

Tyler's account of the story was that she had kept a pet lamb as a child and took it to school with her one day as a dare from her brother. At that time, Roulstone was working as a visiting teacher at her school while preparing to make the move to educational college. He became so captivated by Mary's pet that at the end of the day's schooling he went home, composed the rhyme, and brought it to her the following morning. "He rode across the fields on horseback, to the little old schoolhouse," Tyler later recalled, "and handed me a slip of paper, which had written upon it the three original stanzas of the poem."

The truth of Tyler's version of the story has never been fully established, and Hale remains the rhyme's credited author. Nevertheless, Tyler's hometown of Sterling, Massachusetts, supports her side of this unusual story. It is now home to a plaque and a small statue of Mary's lamb, which stands in the center of the town. Will evidence supporting Tyler's, rather than Hale's, claim of the rhyme's authorship emerge in the future?

Words For Snow

You've probably heard the story about how the Inuit peoples of the high Arctic have 50 different words for snow.

It's a claim that seems to make perfect sense. After all, not all snow is the same - some of it is light and fluffy, some of it is thick and blinding, or slushy, compacted, heavy, slippery, or even liable to give way, or collapse altogether in an avalanche. Having unique words for all those different forms of something that, to the rest of us, we only encounter a few months out of the year appears logical.

However, this is an infamous claim that has yet to be backed up by much in the way of real linguistic evidence. Where the claim first emerged, meanwhile, has never been entirely figured out, and it seems unlikely it was ever the work of anyone with real-world contact with the Inuit peoples. In 2015, however, linguists at the University of Glasgow announced some extraordinary research that led to the Scots language rivaling any claim the Inuit peoples' languages could ever hope to match. Bizarrely, Scotland has more than 400 words for snow.

The Glasgow researchers were working on an online *Historical Thesaurus of Scots*, published as part of the university's landmark Dictionaries of the Scots Language - or rather, *Dictionars o' the Scots Leid* - project. In compiling the thesaurus, the linguists combed several centuries of literature and dictionaries. They uncovered some 421 individual Scots words for different forms of snow.

The words the project unearthed covered almost every eventuality, from a blinding blizzard to the thawing of the winter's snow in spring. So, snow that is said to *feefle* swirls in the wind as it falls. A *fyole* is a light dusting of snow, while a *flindrikin* is a slight or passing snow shower. A *blin-drift* is a mound of drifting snow. A *skovin* is a noticeably big snowflake, while *flukra* is powdery snow that falls in large individual flakes. If the weather is *sneesling*, then it's only just beginning to rain or snow. While the seasonal thawing of frozen snow or land is known as the *unbrak*.

Quite why Scots has so many words for snow was ascribed to the Scottish climate and geography. With so many tall mountains, located at so northerly a latitude, Scotland endures one of the snowiest winters of all European countries. It ranks among the likes of Sweden, Romania, and Alpine Switzerland for the number of days recording snowfall per year.

Writing On The Beaches

Look back through the history books - and through the celebrity autobiographies - and you'll find many famous faces were involved in some way with the wars and battles of the 20th century.

It's a Wonderful Life star James Stewart famously joined the US Air Corps at the outset of his career and in the lead-up to the Second World War. He flew more than 1,800 hours in bomber missions. At the age of 40, Hollywood icon Clark Gable famously volunteered for the US Army Air Forces too and flew in several combat missions as a tail gunner in wartime Germany. Elvis Presley was famously drafted into the US Army at the height of his career in 1958 and served for two years in the US military under the official army serial number 53310761. And before her career in Hollywood, even Audrey Hepburn found a wartime role for herself as a member of the Dutch Resistance.

Of all the names and stories on this wartime list, however, one of the most extraordinary is that of *Catcher in the Rye* author JD Salinger.

Jerome David Salinger was born in New York in 1919. He was busy trying to establish himself as a writer (and romance the Broadway actress Oona O'Neill, daughter of playwright Eugene O'Neill) when in 1942, at the age of 23, he was drafted into the United States Army and sent to war-torn Europe. Able to speak French and German, Salinger was of use not only on the battlefield but was also assigned to counter-intelligence and interpretation services. He was involved in interrogating German prisoners of war and would eventually go on to take part in the liberation of the concentration camp at Dachau.

At the time of his draft, the events of the Second World War had already derailed Salinger's burgeoning career. He had written a story the previous year about a disaffected teenager struggling to understand the events of pre-war America, *Slight Rebellion off Madison*. It had initially been accepted for publication before being suddenly deemed "unpublishable" after Japan attacked Pearl Harbor in December 1941. Devastated, Salinger was forced to shelve the story and was in the middle of reworking it when his army draft papers came through. Faced with little alternative, he took his copy of the story with him to Europe, and continued working on it as and when he could between military operations. Slowly, it began to evolve into a novella, and Salinger gave it a new title, *Catcher in the Rye*.

By now it was 1944, and with the war spiraling to an end in Europe, Salinger found himself embroiled in the Normandy Landings. Salinger and his fellow troops stormed up the beaches of northern France on the morning of D-Day, June

6, 1944. Incredibly, he had the first few draft chapters of *Catcher in the Rye* - the multi-million-selling story by which he would eventually become world-famous - in his backpack as he ran toward the German guns on Utah Beach. Mercifully, he survived the ordeal and after seeing further fighting in both the Battle of the Bulge and the climactic Battle of Hürtgen Forest, returned to America. *Catcher in the Rye* was at long last published to enormous acclaim in 1951.

And The Winner Is...

Nowadays, the highlight of the Hollywood year is the annual Academy Awards. Hosted by the Academy of Motion Picture Arts and Sciences every year since 1929 - when the silent movie *Wings* took home the inaugural Best Picture award - the Oscars have understandably changed a great deal over their long and illustrious history.

The original 1929 ceremony, for instance, lasted a breezy 15 minutes. Bizarrely, those attending to pick up their awards had been informed a full three months earlier that they had won!

Revealing the winners long before the actual ceremony, however, proved something of a dud: there were no surprise announcements, and no shocked and impromptu speech-givers. So, the following year, the Academy changed the rules and kept the winning actors and filmmakers a surprise until the night of the ceremony. The only people who were permitted to know who the winners would be ahead of time were the press so that they could write up their copy in advance ahead of their morning edition.

That system worked perfectly for the next decade or so, until the night of the 1940 Oscars ceremony. This was the first time that the awards were to be filmed. With all eyes (and all cameras) on Hollywood, a lavish gala event, hosted for the first time by showbusiness legend Bob Hope, was arranged in one of the town's favorite celebrity haunts, the Coconut Grove.

This was to be the first Academy Awards of a new celebrity era, with A-list stars arriving at the Grove in tuxedos and evening gowns, and cameras capturing every speech and winning announcement in exquisite detail. Unfortunately, someone spoiled it.

As had always been the case before then, the press had once again been informed ahead of time who the winners of the 1940s Oscars were to be. An embargo (ban) was imposed by the Academy preventing the publication of their names until 11 p.m. that night, long after the ceremony had been concluded. Keen to get a scoop on such an important night, however, the *Los Angeles Times* broke the embargo. They published all the winning names in their early evening edition, so everyone arriving at the Cocoanut Grove could pick up a copy of the paper in the lobby, and see whether or not they were to win.

The *Times* may have gotten the scoop, but the Academy was furious. With the most lavish night in its history effectively ruined, the rules were changed once and for all. By the 1941 Oscars, there were to be no prior announcements whatsoever, meaning the press and the winners would all find out at the same time. As a result, sealed envelopes were incorporated into the ceremony for the very first time, and the surprise "And the Oscar goes too…" moment was born.

Cataracts And Hurricanoes

It is one of Shakespeare's most popular plays and one of the last on which he ever worked. *The Tempest* tells the story of a mercurial sorcerer, Prospero, and the misfit band of survivors of a shipwreck - including Prospero's estranged brother Antonio, the usurper Duke of Milan. They find themselves washed up on his island of magic, spirits, and monsters. Shakespeare may have made these monsters and spirits up, of course, but when it came to writing *The Tempest*, he did at least take inspiration from one extraordinary real-world event.

In June 1609, a ship named the *Sea Venture* set sail from Portsmouth, on the south coast of England. It was part of a fleet of ships heading for England's colonies at Jamestown, Virginia. On board were 150 passengers and crew, and the ship's captain, an experienced mariner named Sir George Somers.

After just over seven weeks at sea, however, in July the fleet sailed directly into an enormous mid-Atlantic hurricane. Other ships in the company managed to successfully weave their way around it and head north to escape the storm. However, the *Sea Venture* became separated from the rest of the fleet amid the gales and churning seas. It found itself heading directly into the hurricane's eye, alone.

Captain Somers knew he had few options. To survive the hurricane, he and his crew had to find land, and there seek a safe harbor in which to ride out the storm. In desperation, he ultimately steered the ship toward the only land he and the *Sea Venture* had seen for weeks. He intentionally ran the ship aground in a rocky, low-lying inlet on the coast of Bermuda. The decision was a drastic one, but the right one: all 150 people on board survived.

Having wrecked the ship in order to escape the storm, however, Somers and the other survivors were now marooned and remained stranded on Bermuda for the next nine months. Eventually, having seen out the winter, Somers and his men used the wreckage of the *Sea Venture* - as well as new timbers sourced from the island - to build two smaller vessels. They christened these '*Deliverance* and *Patience*'. At long last, they could all set sail once more, and the group finally arrived in Jamestown almost a year to the day after they departed England, on May 23, 1610.

News of Somers' quick-thinking and ingenuity reached home several weeks later, and the story of the *Sea Venture's* remarkable survival caused a sensation in Elizabethan England - and inspired Shakespeare to begin work on *The Tempest*.

Today, as well as giving us one of the greatest plays in the theatrical canon of English literature, the ordeal of the *Sea*

Venture is also immortalized on the flag and the coat of arms of Bermuda. The central field of the flag depicts a large sailing ship being wrecked amid stormy seas.

That's A Rap

Cinema has given us some terrifying villains over the years, from memorable movie adaptations like *Dracula* and *Frankenstein* to *A Nightmare on Elm Street*'s Freddy Krueger, the *Halloween* franchise's Michael Myers, and *Friday the 13th*'s Jason Voorhees. But when it comes to big-screen monsters, few are quite so memorable - nor quite so subtly terrifying - as the super-intelligent velociraptors of Steven Spielberg's *Jurassic Park*.

When it came to adapting Michael Crichton's best-selling thriller for the big screen in 1993, Spielberg's team knew that a complex mix of animatronics and computer-generated special effects would be required to make the dinosaurs come to life. Each of the creatures in the story went through countless designs and redesigns during preproduction. Finally, the special effects team arrived at an utterly seamless blend of real-life puppetry and state-of-the-art CGI. As the film critic Leonard Maltin wrote in his rave review at the time, "The dinosaurs seem *alive*."

Making a puppet or CGI monster *move* like a real creature on screen is one thing - making them *sound* realistic is another.

The sound engineers of *Jurassic Park* knew that their work would be just as important for making the dinosaurs seem as realistic as possible. However, with no clue as to what a dinosaur actually sounds like, it is fair to say they had their work cut out. In the end, the team arrived at a remarkable solution. Rather than make, record, or digitally manipulate a single sound to produce a T-rex's roar or a velociraptor's screech, they combined and overlayed the sounds of multiple animals. This created an utterly unique sound no one would have ever heard in nature before.

The roar of a bull elephant, for instance, was mixed with the resonating growls of a tiger and an alligator to create the bellow of the Tyrannosaurus rex (while its breath was made from the sound of a whale blowing air from its blowhole, and its footsteps were the sound of giant sequoias being felled and crashing to the ground). The Gallimimus dinosaurs' high-pitched screams as they flee the Tyrannosaur were likewise based on the high-pitched neigh of a female horse. And the croaks, trills, and screeches of the monstrous tar-spitting Dilophosaurus were concocted from a bizarre mix of a cooing swan, a calling hawk, and a hissing rattlesnake.

When it came to the velociraptors, however, the sound design team had an even bigger challenge. In the movie, the raptors are seldom seen on screen until toward the end of the movie, and so sound alone is used to hint at how monstrous they truly are. Not only that but the velociraptors are portrayed as hunting together - as if in a pack. This meant they not only needed to produce terrifying screams as they attack their prey but also softer calls and sounds as they bark at and communicate with one another.

In the end, the raptors' voices were pieced together from an extraordinary cocktail of sounds: the breathy neigh of a worn-out horse; a squealing dolphin in heat; the hiss of an enraged goose (the eerie sound that can be heard when the hidden raptor surprises the game hunter Robert Muldoon); and even the low, rumbling bark of a mating tortoise. For all their extraordinarily effective efforts, the filmmakers were amply awarded: *Jurassic Park* won all three of the technical Academy Awards for which it was nominated in 1994, including the awards for Best Sound Editing, Best Sound Mixing, and Best Visual Effects.

A Shocking History

You'll no doubt have heard the famous tale of Benjamin Franklin rushing out into a summer thunderstorm holding a child's kite. According to the story, attached to the kite was a small metal object (usually said to have been a key). With this item, Franklin was said to be attempting to collect an ambient electrical charge from the storm clouds above, to prove the connection between natural lightning and generated electricity.

The truth of the story of Franklin's kite experiment is debatable. Some claim that the entire story is fictitious, while others suggest it is a gross exaggeration and Franklin merely suggested the idea, heard of others who had done it, or else tried to collect a charge this way yet failed. What is true, though, is that Franklin - as one of the greatest minds of his day - was indeed fascinated by electricity, and by how its power could be harnessed.

Franklin's electrical experiments began in the mid-1740s; his kite experiment is usually said to have taken place during a thunderstorm in July 1752. "I never was before engaged in any study that so totally engrossed my attention and my time, as this has lately done," Franklin wrote to a friend and fellow polymath (a person of wide knowledge or learning), Peter Collinson, in 1745. Collinson had sent Franklin a Leyden jar - a glass canister capable of storing a high-voltage electric charge. Franklin had soon become obsessed with using the charge inside it in his research.

Franklin's Leyden jar experiments came to a head in 1749. He hosted a party at which he served his guests a whole turkey on an electric barbecue and served wine from goblets containing tiny electrical charges so that they shocked the drinker every time they took a sip. Staying fully on the theme, Franklin killed the turkey using electrocution.

He tried to repeat the successes of the previous year's banquet the following Christmas, by electrocuting a holiday turkey he intended to serve to his guests at a festive party at his home. This time, however, the experiment didn't quite go to plan and Franklin almost killed himself instead. "I have lately made an experiment in electricity that I desire never to repeat," he later wrote. "Being about to kill a turkey by the shock from two large glass [Leyden] jars...I inadvertently took the whole through my own arms and body."

Having heard a loud crack and seen a flash of light, Franklin's guests entered the kitchen to find him standing in the middle of the room trembling and looking decidedly dazed. The shock had all but wiped his short-term memory, and he had no recollection of the accident at all. "The first thing I took notice of was a violent, quick shaking of my body," he explained, "which, gradually remitting, my sense [just] as gradually returned."

Happily, there were no long-term consequences of Franklin's accidental electrocution, aside from some tremors and soreness that eased over the following weeks. In fact,

Franklin is said to have later admitted that the only long-term damage was to his pride!

Did You Know?

The Stories Behind Seven More Movie Sound Effects

○ **TRON**

To produce the bizarre whizzing sound of the light-cycles in 1982's science fiction hit *Tron*, a series of electronic beeps and whistles from early computers and video game systems were warped and overlayed one on top of the other. Then, to give the sound a harsher and more industrial edge, the noise made by an electric buzz saw was thrown into the mix as well.

○ **THE LORD OF THE RINGS**

Just as in *Jurassic Park*, when it came to making the sound of the legendary monsters and creatures in Peter Jackson's *Lord of the Rings* films, the sound team had to come up with a sound no one had ever heard before. Chief amongst them was the gigantic fire-breathing Balrog, which emerges from the depths of an ancient mountain to do battle with the wizard Gandalf. To create the sound of a creature made of rock and flames waking from its slumber after an endless number of years, cinderblocks were recorded as being dragged along a wooden floor. And the Balrog's roar as it finally catches up with Gandalf at the Bridge of Khazad-Dûm? A warped mixture of a bellowing horse and a bellowing donkey.

○ **GHOSTBUSTERS**

In the original 1980s *Ghostbusters* franchise, the sound of the electronic proton packs - the ray guns used to trap and control the movie's ghosts - was reportedly made by slowing down and filtering the sound of an electric engine turbine.

○ **STAR WARS**

Like all sci-fi movies, 1977's *Star Wars* required an entire engine room of futuristic-sounding computerized beeps and tones to bring the movie to life. Originally, that soundscape of high-pitched bleeps and bloops even extended to the film's main villain, Darth Vader. Held together by a complex walking life-support system, in early rough cuts of the movie, Vader was accompanied on screen by a series of noises like those heard in an operating theatre. Thankfully, the filmmakers reconsidered that approach, ditched the beeps and whirrs, and decided to give Darth Vader a much more menacing sound. The inside of a hospital ventilator was recorded as someone took a series of deep inhalations and exhalations, and then the sound was slowed and manipulated to create Vader's characteristic death-rattle breaths.

○ STAR WARS (AGAIN!)

Besides Darth Vader's breathing, perhaps the most iconic sound effect in the *Star Wars* franchise is the electronic whirring and buzzing of the main character's light sabras. To create the sound, the movie's sound designers combined the hum of an old television set as it warmed up with the whirring buzz of a running cinema projector. Then, to make the sounds grow and fade as the sabers are swung back and forth mid-battle, the combined sounds played via an old speaker system while the microphone recording them was whirled around in a circle.

○ GODZILLA

Godzilla has appeared in dozens of films since its debut appearance more than six decades ago in the original Japanese movie in 1954. Although Godzilla's roar has changed somewhat over the years, the original Japanese sound designers initially struggled when it came to providing it with a voice for its first on-screen appearance. None of the combinations of barks, roars, screeches, and other animal noises they tested seemed quite to fit. It was at that point that the movie's composer Akira Ifukube stepped in with a much more hands-on approach - quite literally in fact! The bellowing sound of Godzilla's roar in the original movie was created by one of the sound team putting on a leather glove, painting it with pine resin, and then running it down the string of a double bass.

PSYCHO

We've already found out about how Alfred Hitchcock orchestrated the infamous shower scene in 1960s *Psycho*, but what about the sound in the scene? Bernard Hermann's famous score is the most well-known, although Hitchcock originally did not want to use it, preferring instead to keep the scene silent. Besides the score though, the director used his own series of makeshift sounds to expertly grisly effect. Although the audience never actually sees the knife blade stab Marion Crane as she stands in the shower, we hear the sound of the knife cutting her flesh numerous times, leaving the squeamish brutality of her death entirely up to our imagination (and doubtless making the scene all the more effective). As much as it might sound like someone being cut to pieces, however, the sound you're *actually* hearing is Alfred Hitchcock jamming a knife into a casaba melon.

The Lost Prince

The royal history of France is surely one of the most tumultuous in the world. From beheadings to madness, the lives of many of the kings and queens of France make for truly remarkable and dramatic tales - perhaps none more so than that of the tragic and doomed Revolutionary queen, Marie Antoinette.

The daughter of the Holy Roman Emperor, Marie Antoinette married her husband, the heir to the French throne, Louis-Auguste, in 1770. At the time, she was just 14 years old. In 1774, the French King Louis XV died, and Marie Antoinette's husband rose to succeed him as Louis XVI - and in doing so, she assumed the title of Queen of France.

At the outbreak of the French Revolution in 1789, however, attitudes toward the royal family soured, and Louis and Marie were soon imprisoned along with their children. The king was sent to the guillotine in the January of 1793, whereafter Marie Antoinette found herself likewise charged with high treason, and subject to a two-day sham trial. Eventually, she too was sentenced to death and followed her husband to the guillotine on 14 October. But incredibly, the drama of her life was to continue, even after her untimely death.

The king and queen's surviving children were spared their parents' fate, though, in post-Revolutionary France, none had a particularly good or happy life. Princess Marie Thérèse, the couple's eldest child, went on to marry and become the Duchess of Angoulême. However, such was the political landscape at the time that she was compelled to spend much of her life in exile. She was still banished at the time of her death in 1851.

The couple's eldest son, Louis Joseph, the dauphin of France, had died in childhood shortly before the outbreak of the revolution and had ultimately passed his claim to the French throne over to his younger brother, Louis Charles. In the eyes of the staunch French Royalists, at least, Louis Charles went on to become the rightful King Louis XVII of France after his father's execution in 1793. Yet when the Republic was installed, Louis' claim to the throne was never fully acknowledged.

It is now generally understood that Louis Charles, like his brother, also passed away in childhood, having likely contracted tuberculosis that was rife in the prisons where he and his family were kept. But the mystery surrounding the precise details of his life for a long time left a gap in the historical record. Many people were all too keen to fill that gap with rumor, presumption, and deception. As a result, many people in 19th-century France believed the young boy king to still be alive, and that like his older sister, he was merely living in exile, awaiting the reinstitution of the monarchy.

As time wore on, ever more people subscribed to this unfounded conspiracy theory - and ever more men stepped forward to dubiously claim that *they* were the long-lost king of France, Louis Charles, and the rightful heir to the French throne. In fact, over the next century, more than 100 men claimed to be the missing king Louis XVII. Not all of them were quite so equally believed, of course. Many of these pretenders to the throne had their claims immediately quashed and debunked. But at least one of them found considerable support.

In the mid-1830s, a German clockmaker named Karl Wilhelm Naundorff arrived in post-Revolutionary Paris claiming to be Marie Antoinette's son, Louis Charles. Unlike many other long-lost claimants to the throne, Naundorff somehow managed to gain the support of several high-society Royalist Parisians, all of whom advocated that his story was true. Chief among them was Louis' former governess, who believed Naundorff to be so physically similar to the young prince that his tale must surely be true.

Despite this, however, Naundorff never produced any solid proof of his supposed identity and was eventually dismissed as a fraud and ejected from the country. He died in the Netherlands in 1845, professing until the very end that he was indeed the rightful king of France. He appeared so sure, in fact, that many Dutch people continued to support his claim and view him as wronged by history long after his death.

At long last, the issue was finally put to rest with the advent of DNA evidence. In 2017 - after more than 150 years of inconclusive and controversial tests - it was finally established once and for all that Naundorff's tale had been a lie. One of the most bizarre chapters in French history was finally over, and the tragic queen whose life and death had instigated all this upheaval could finally rest in peace.

Help Is On The Way

The renowned British–Irish explorer Sir Ernest Shackleton is known for three groundbreaking polar expeditions he oversaw in 1907, 1914, and 1921.

Shackleton first got a taste for polar exploration while serving as third officer on board his fellow explorer Captain Robert Falcon Scott's ship, the *Discovery*, in 1901. Six years later, he launched his own *Nimrod* expedition. In January 1909, he set a new record by trekking to a southern latitude of 88° - eventually coming within just 97 miles of the South Pole. During the same trip, members of his *Nimrod* crew also succeeded in reaching the magnetic South Pole and climbing the highest mountain in Antarctica, Mount Erebus. For all the '*Nimrod's*' remarkable achievements, Shackleton was knighted by King Edward VII on his return home to England.

In 1914, Shackleton set off for a second time for the Southern Ocean as part of what became known as the Imperial Trans-Antarctic Expedition. This time, however, he and his crew would have far less luck.

On their arrival in Antarctica in October 1915, disaster struck almost immediately when Shackleton's ship, the *Endurance*, became trapped in pack ice in the Weddell Sea and was slowly crushed to pieces. As the ship went down, Shackleton and his crew of 27 men were forced to lower themselves down onto the surrounding sea ice in the ship's lifeboats. Having grabbed whatever equipment and provisions they could carry from the ship; they camped out on top of the floe. Without sufficient gear to launch the expedition they had planned, the men were forced to remain on the ice floe as it slowly drifted northward, with no solid land - nor indeed any means of rescue or escape - in sight.

By the following spring, the ice had begun to break apart, and Shackleton and his men had to flee the ice in the three surviving lifeboats. Now out in the open ocean, they headed as best they could toward the closest solid land, Elephant Island. Named for the large population of elephant seals that inhabit it, the men's arrival on the island at least meant that they had a ready supply of fresh meat, and so were now no longer doomed to starve. But that still left them stranded on an isolated rock, in the middle of the roughest seas on the planet, with no means of escape!

Eventually, Shackleton decided that their only chance of rescue was to take the most seaworthy of the three lifeboats, the *James Caird*, and set off once again into the Southern Ocean. He hoped they could land at the nearby larger island of South Georgia. It was known to have several manned whaling stations and was therefore their best chance of ensuring rescue and a safe passage home. Unfortunately, the journey there would entail crossing more than 800 miles of rough seas, in nothing more than an open wooden lifeboat.

Incredibly - despite almost capsizing several times and rowing straight into a hurricane-force storm - Shackleton and a handpicked crew of six men survived the journey. They arrived on the southern coast of South Georgia 17 days later. From there, three of the party trekked across the island and scaled its enormous central mountain to arrive at the closest whaling station on the north coast. Once there, the rescue of the remaining crewmen back on Elephant Island could be arranged, and the entire ordeal could at long last be concluded. By 1917, Shackleton was back in London - and before long, was organizing his third and final polar expedition.

The so-called Shackleton–Rowett Expedition launched in 1921. Delayed by problems with the new ship, the *Quest*, and by hostile seas in the mid-Atlantic, this time it took longer than expected for Shackleton and his men to reach the Southern Ocean. Unfortunately, on January 5, 1922, he died suddenly of a heart attack on board the *Quest* before the expedition could truly get underway.

In accordance with the wishes of his wife back in England, Emily Dorman, Shackleton was buried on South Georgia - the island that had assured his salvation five years earlier.

From One To The Other

You likely know that the events of the First World War were set in motion, on the morning of June 28, 1914, by the assassination of Archduke Franz Ferdinand. He was the presumed heir to the throne of Austria-Hungary.

Both Ferdinand and his wife, Sophie, the Duchess of Hohenberg, were shot and killed in Sarajevo by a 19-year-old Bosnian Serb activist named Gavrilo Princip. He and the six other men who had coordinated the assassination were members of a secret Serbian student revolutionary organization (later known as Young Bosnia). It was seeking to end Austria-Hungary's rule of the Balkans, and establish a free South Slav state in its place.

The archduke's murder ultimately led to mutual hostilities escalating between a number of European nations and culminated in his native Austria-Hungary declaring war on Princip's Serbia. Just four weeks after his death, the situation had snowballed further to such an extent that all the allies of Austria-Hungary and the allies of Serbia declared war on one another too. This triggered the First World War. The conflict rumbled on across Europe for the next four years and eventually led to the deaths of some 20 million people (a little over half of whom were civilians).

Incredibly, though, this entire tragedy could have played out entirely differently - especially given that the archduke's assassination occurred just minutes after an earlier attempt on his life had failed!

Earlier on the morning of June 28, at around 10.10 a.m., the archduke and his wife were traveling as part of a motorcade through Sarajevo. Another of the assassins in Princip's group, Nedeljko Čabrinović, threw a small hand-held bomb toward their car. The bomb missed its intended targets, however, and bounced off the car's leather hood before falling onto the ground. By the time the timer on the bomb went off, the next car in the archduke's motorcade was directly on top of it. As it exploded, the second car was badly damaged. Around 15 people were injured by the explosion, and a foot-wide crater (likely lessened in size by the car atop of it) was left in the road - though happily, there were no fatalities.

Čabrinović, meanwhile, swallowed a cyanide tablet and threw himself over the side of a nearby bridge into the Miljacka river below. Unfortunately for him, the cyanide pill failed to act effectively (and merely induced intense vomiting). Plus, the Milijacka was so shallow at that time of the year that he landed in scarcely six inches of water. Dazed and injured, Čabrinović was hauled from the river by police and arrested.

The group's attempt on the archduke's life had grossly misfired, and his motorcade continued on its way.

That should have been the end of it. The archduke trundled on down the road and arrived at the local governor's hall where a reception was being held in his honor. Understandably a little shaken, Ferdinand reportedly arrived at the governor's residence angrily exclaiming, "So this is how you welcome your guests? With bombs?!"

When the reception was concluded at around 11.00 a.m., however, the archduke and his wife decided that rather than continuing on their way as planned, they would head back down the street they had just driven up. They wanted to meet with the people who had been injured by the bombing. As the cars backed up along the road, one of them stalled and the motorcade suddenly ground to a halt. It was at this point that Princip - knowing that the bomb had failed and that the rest of the assassins had deserted - saw his chance. He strode across the street, firing twice into the open car.

As a result, the entire course of Europe's history and the lives of some 20 million people depended on little more than a spur-of-the-moment decision and a misfiring engine.

Down, Down, And Upside Down

There are countless tales of survival and endurance against all odds in history books. Surely one of the most extraordinary in recent times took place 100 ft below the surface of the Atlantic Ocean in 2013. Twenty-nine-year-old Harrison Okene was working as the chef on board a tugboat around 20 miles off the coast of Nigeria when the vessel capsized in rough water at around 5 a.m. and began to sink. Okene's 10 fellow crewmembers all drowned in the disaster, but as the ship sank upside down - down to a depth of more than 100 ft to the seabed below - he found himself trapped in an air pocket still in the ship's kitchen.

Okene knew that to survive, he would have to conserve what little air there was in the roughly one-square-meter space above his head. He'd also somehow have to keep himself as clear of the water as possible to stave off hypothermia. He was in pitch darkness and wearing nothing but his underwear, as the disaster had struck so early in the morning. Still, he managed to fashion a makeshift platform to support himself almost entirely above the water and awaited rescue.

Incredibly, Okene endured this torturous ordeal for the next two-and-a-half days. Then a team of rescue divers from

South Africa finally arrived on the scene to check for survivors and retrieve the bodies of those who had perished. As he saw a beam of torchlight slowly moving toward him through the water, Okene reached out and waved. The diver swimming toward him was understandably surprised to find anyone alive in such a precarious position, but the team soon set about rescuing him. That, however, was easier said than done.

After such a long time underwater, and at such an extraordinary depth, Okene could not be immediately returned to the surface without risking decompression sickness (also known as "the bends"). Instead, he had to be loaded into a pressurized diving bell that would allow the gas levels in his body to be carefully monitored and returned to normal. That process took another two grueling days, during which Okene lost consciousness several times - but against all odds, he survived.

Having vowed never to return to sea again, he qualified as a commercial scuba diver in 2015. At the diploma ceremony, the diver whom he had reached out and waved to presented him with his certificate!

Rabbiting On

He may not have succeeded in all his military and political aspirations, but Napoleon Bonaparte nevertheless secured a reputation for himself as one of the most influential figures in history. There is, however, at least one event in his life that he would probably like us to forget - and no, it's not the Battle of Waterloo.

In the summer of 1807, Napoleonic France signed a treaty ending the French Empire's longstanding war with Russia. To celebrate the occasion, Napoleon demanded a vast hunting party be organized, and his imperial chief of staff, Alexandre Berthier, was given the task of putting the event together.

Whether it was Berthier or Napoleon himself who takes the blame for what happened next is unclear. Either way, it proved somewhat embarrassing for the French ruler. Hundreds of (or, by some accounts, as many as 3,000) wild rabbits were rounded up from the local countryside and placed in row upon row of cages along the edges of one of the fields where Napoleon's hunt was due to take place. As he and his men set off, the plan was to open the cages and free the rabbits, which would then vanish into the undergrowth from where they could be caught. Unfortunately, when the call came to open the cages, the rabbits didn't simply hop out and scurry away - they leapt out and ran in their hundreds across the open ground, directly toward Napoleon!

At first, he and his men reportedly saw the funny side of what was happening, and simply laughed at the sight of a few thousand rabbits hurtling toward them. But as the creatures made a beeline for Napoleon, his laughter quickly turned to panic. The animals began trying to climb up his legs and leaping up to grab his belt and breeches. Now far too close to get a clean shot with a gun, Napoleon tried vainly to push the animals off with his riding crop, but there were simply too many to deal with. Before long, he was at risk of being knocked to the ground and swamped.

In desperation, he fled back to his carriage - but still the rabbits kept coming. They swarmed the path ahead of his coach, making it all but impossible to make a swift getaway. Some accounts claim that a few of the rabbits even managed to leap up and climb into the coach itself. Eventually, the coach was able to get moving, leaving a somewhat shaken Napoleon to make a slow and (somewhat humiliated) exit.

It was Berthier's fault. Rather than trapping wild hares, his men had bought tame rabbits from local farmers. As a result, the rabbits didn't see Napoleon as a fearsome hunter. They saw him as a waiter bringing out the day's food. To them, the emperor was effectively a giant head of lettuce.

L'inconnue De La Seine

In the late 1880s, the body of a beautiful but unknown young woman—perhaps no more than 20 years old - was pulled out of the River Seine, in central Paris. Her body was taken to the local mortuary, where the Paris police attempted to identify her. A pathologist was called on to figure out her cause of death. Although there were no signs of foul play or violence - and so her cause of death was listed as a tragic suicide - the officers found nothing at all by which to identify her. As a consequence, she had to go unnamed in their reports. As the case was reported in the press, she became known as l'Inconnue de la Seine—literally, 'the Seine's Unknown.'

According to Paris lore, the pathologist in charge of her case at the mortuary was reportedly so taken by the girl's youth and her beauty that he took a plaster cast of her face. He was determined to do right by her death and at least track down her name and family. Taking a cast meant that, even after her burial, he could continue to try to find someone who may recognize her. As the case rumbled inconclusively on and the city-wide search intensified, ever more plaster copies of the girl's death mask began to be made. Yet still, no one in the city seemed to know who she was, and the case remained unsolved.

Eventually, however, so many copies of the girl's face had been produced that the masks ceased to serve their original purpose. Before long, they began to appear elsewhere: on the walls of artists' studios to be used as a reference guide for drawing faces, and even in the city's flea markets and book stalls, where they were sold as morbid curios to Paris' Bohemian writers and musicians.

The girl's face gradually became an icon of turn-of-the-century culture. She was the subject of early photographs and paintings, and references to her death mask appear in dozens of contemporary songs, poems, plays, and literature. She even became so well known that in 1900, the English writer Richard Le Gallienne published a novel, *The Worshipper of the Image*, telling the story of a lovelorn poet who falls in love with the Inconnue mask, and suffers a tragic downfall as his obsession overwhelms his life.

In one final and bizarre twist to this morbid story, in 1960 the girl's mask was used as the model for *Resusci Anne*. That's a plastic mannequin on which medical students and first aid practitioners could learn and practice the techniques of artificial respiration. The *Anne* simulator has since become the standard model for CPR dummies the world over, with models produced and sold across Europe, Australia, and North America. The Inconnue of the Seine may still be unidentified, but she is now surely one of the most well-known faces in the world.

Did You Know?

Seven More John and Jane Does from History

○ **THE LADY OF THE DUNES**

In 1974, the disfigured body of a woman - estimated to be somewhere between 25 and 49 years old - was found half buried in the sand dunes at Cape Cod. Her identity has never been found out (even when the case was recently reopened and modern DNA techniques employed). Further, it has never been explained how she came to die, how she ended up on the beach, and how she came to be buried in the sand dunes.

○ **THE TAMÁM SHUD MAN**

In 1948, an unidentified man's body was found on Somerton Beach in South Australia. In the man's pocket was a page torn from a copy of *The Rubaiyat of Omar Khayyam*, a collection of Persian poems translated into English in 1859. On the page, the phrase *tamám shud* - literally meaning 'ended' or 'over' - had been highlighted. Australian police investigating the mysterious case eventually found the actual copy of the book from which the page had been torn. Inside was scrawled an unknown telephone number and a series of bizarre symbols. It was popularly presumed that he was a Cold War spy, that the scribbled writings and indentations were part of some kind of code, and that the *Rubaiyat* was the set text from which he and his fellow infiltrators could decipher the encrypted messages sent to one another. DNA evidence reported in 2022, however, identified the Somerton man as an electrical engineer and instrument maker called Carl "Charles" Webb, who'd lived a troubled yet quite ordinary life.

○ THE TROW GHYLL SKELETON

In 1947, a skeleton was discovered by two potholers in a cave close to Trow Ghyll, a vast limestone gorge in West Yorkshire, England. The identity of the body has never been confirmed, but it is popularly claimed that the remains were those of a German spy. If so, the Trow Ghyll skeleton is said to be the most telling evidence available that a network of Nazi German agents had indeed infiltrated English society during the Second World War.

○ GREEN BOOTS

"Green Boots" is the name given to the unidentified body of a climber wearing green mountaineering boots that was found inside a cave on the northeast ridge of Mount Everest - at a height of approximately 28,000 ft - in 1996. Because of the body's location, it has never been possible to remove it. Although a team of Chinese climbers dragged the body to a less conspicuous location in 2014, Green Boots has since become a kind of grisly landmark for anyone scaling Everest along the same ridge. Although many suggestions claiming to have identified the body have been made over the year, none has been officially accepted.

BELLA IN THE WYCH-ELM

One of the eeriest cold cases in British criminal history took place in 1943 when a group of schoolboys stumbled across the body of a woman stuffed inside a hollow Wych-elm tree in the town of Stourbridge, near Birmingham. It was estimated the body had been there for over a year before it was discovered. The case understandably caused a sensation, and although the woman's body could not be identified, within a matter of days odd messages and graffiti began turning up on walls and monuments in the town, asking "Who put Bella in the Wych-elm?" The identity of "Bella" - and how she came to such a gruesome and bizarre end—has never been resolved.

LITTLE MISS PANASOFFKEE

In 1971, the body of a young woman who had been strangled was found beneath Lake Panasoffkee bridge in Sumter County, Florida. Police were unable to identify her, and her killer was never found. The case was reopened in 2012 and some intriguing new clues have been identified using modern investigative techniques. DNA evidence suggested the woman was of Greek heritage, had likely given birth at some point, had had extensive reconstructive dental work, and had undergone ankle surgery. Despite all of these additional identifying factors, however, the woman's case remains unsolved after more than 50 years. The identity of "Little Miss Panasoffkee," as she has become known, remains unknown.

○ THE EL DORADO JANE DOE

One of the most famous unidentified cases of recent years is that of El Dorado Jane Doe. She was shot and killed in a motel in El Dorado, Arkansas, by James "Ice" McAlphin in July 1991. Despite police identifying her killer - and managing to track down many of the deceased woman's friends (and even now, using DNA evidence, her family) - the woman's true identity has never been discovered. At the time of her death, all her friends who spoke to the police gave different names and different accounts of her life. Further, all the woman's blood relatives who have been identified by police were entirely unaware of their connection to the case.

Late To The Party

The history books are full of stories of Japanese Second World War troops that, due to finding themselves stranded on isolated islands in the Pacific Ocean, never hear a word of the war being over, and continue fighting when rescued or discovered many years later.

Famously, 2nd Lieutenant Hiroo Onoda hid out on an island in the Philippines and did not surrender for 29 years. In 2005, two Japanese men - both then in their 80s - were discovered living in the jungles and mountains of the island of Mindanao, supposedly unaware that the war had ended 60 years earlier. But Japan was not the only Axis power whose troops failed to accept or acknowledge the end of the war.

With the war drawing to a close and defeat seeming imminent, on May 5, 1945, German Admiral Karl Dönitz sent an order from Berlin that all German submarines were to stand down and return to port. Positioned off the north coast of Scotland at the time, however, U-boat *U-977* - under the control of *Oberleutnant* Heinz Schäffer - refused to accept the order. Instead, Schäffer decided to take the submarine across the Atlantic Ocean, and escape to Argentina.

It has long been suggested that Schäffer thought the message from Dönitz was fake and had been sent by British intelligence as a trick to force any German U-boats in British waters to the surface. In an interrogation session later, however, Schäffer revealed that not to be the case.

Instead, he and his men believed the war to be over, yet were fearful of their treatment as prisoners of war and of what may become of their homeland in the event of a German defeat. He offered any of the crew who wished to leave the submarine in Europe the chance to do so (16 men opted to depart in dinghies and landed on Holsnøy island in Norway five days later). Then Schäffer headed south to Argentina, knowing that it had a relatively large German expatriate community.

The 9,000-mile journey took 99 days, and U-977 is popularly said to have completed one of the longest undersea missions of the entire Second World War (albeit, long after the war had actually ended). Unfortunately, Schäffer's plan did not entirely work out. After surrendering to the Argentine authorities, he and his crew were extradited to the United States and sent back to Europe for questioning. They spent the next two years in custody but were released in 1947.

Acting Up

He may be one of the world's greatest novelists, but Charles Dickens was really a frustrated actor.

Before he took up a career in literature, Dickens longed to work in the theatre. As an avid fan of the stage, at one point during his time in London, he claimed to have gone to the theatre every day for three years! He spent his free time alongside his first professional employment - working as a junior legal clerk in the late 1820s at the offices of an attorney in Holborn, London - learning the speeches and monologues of his favorite West End stars. He was a gifted mimic too and would entertain his fellow clerks by doing impressions of their bosses, all the time honing his skills as a comic, which he hoped one day to bring to the stage himself. Eventually, in 1832, he plucked up the courage to make a go of his long-held ambition and put his name down for an audition in a Covent Garden theatre.

Unfortunately, it wasn't to be. On the morning of the audition, Dickens awoke with a terrible head cold. Feeling woozy and unwell, he was forced to miss the audition. The part went to a different aspiring actor, and Dickens put his ambitions to one side.

At around the same time, however, Dickens was becoming a more skilled and accomplished writer. He had begun writing works for the stage rather than looking to perform on it himself. In 1836, he wrote his first play, *The Strange Gentlemen*, and even a comic opera, entitled *The Village Coquettes*.

1836 was also the year in which Dickens published his first novel, *The Pickwick Papers*. Its immediate success took him away from the stage and into full-time literary writing. When the final installment of the novel went to print the following year, Dickens started work almost immediately on his second novel, *Oliver Twist*. Within a matter of months, he was the country's most celebrated new author.

Although a stellar career in literature was now all but guaranteed, Dickens nevertheless appears to have longed for a life on the stage. While on a tour of Canada in the 1840s, he even took the opportunity to appear in a handful of plays, which were well-received by critics and audiences at the time. His stage successes never outshone his literary works, however - and given how popular and much-loved his books have become, it's perhaps a good thing for us that they didn't!

Two's Company

Picture the high-society ladies of Georgian England, and you'll probably have an image of some graceful Jane Austen-style heroine in your mind. Admittedly, the *last* thing on your mind will probably be an insult-ridden argument between two such ladies. Yet according to a late 18th-century edition of the London magazine *Carlton House*, there was at least one unfortunate event in which two upmarket Georgian ladies violently and somewhat spectacularly fell out.

It was in 1792 that a lady identified only as Mrs Elphinstone paid a visit to her friend Lady Almeria Braddock in central London. The two were casually catching up over tea and sandwiches when Mrs Elphinstone happened casually to comment that Lady Braddock had once been "a very beautiful woman." Lady Braddock was quick to react.

"What do you mean, that I have *been* beautiful?" she asked. Noticing that she was on decidedly uneasy ground, Mrs Elphinstone tried to cushion her comments by explaining that Lady Braddock now had a "good autumn face," and that although still beautiful today, her "lilies and roses are somewhat faded" compared to how she had looked some 40 years ago. Despite her best efforts, however, Mrs Elphinstone had quite clearly dug a conversational hole - and expanding on her comments was only digging deeper.

The pair's argument spiraled out of control, with Lady Braddock claiming to still be in her thirties, despite Mrs Elphinstone having good evidence that she was well past 60. Lady Braddock finally decided to call out her sparring partner and challenged Mrs Elphinstone to a duel. The pair met soon after in Hyde Park, armed with pistols.

Their shots fired, Mrs Elphinstone succeeded only in shooting a hole through Lady Braddock's hat, and other than that, the two were unharmed. Still refusing to back down and apologize, the pair next set to with sabers. This time, Lady Braddock managed to strike her opponent first, inflicting a small wound on her right arm. With each now having effectively struck the other, honor was considered restored, and the matter was declared closed.

In the decades since the precise events of the so-called "Petticoat Duel" of 1792 have been questioned. Some historians now believe that the magazine's record of the event was either somewhat exaggerated or entirely fictitious. Precisely what the truth behind the tale really is, unfortunately, will likely never be known for sure.

Odd One Out

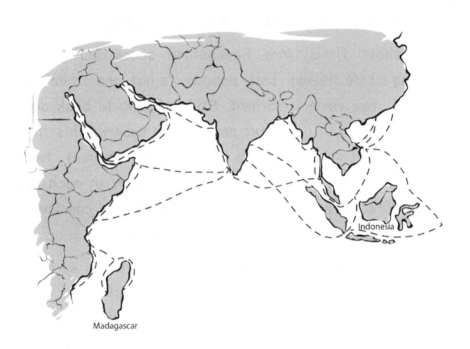

Languages are a lot like the people that speak them. Often, those that interact and are found geographically nearby one another tend to be more closely related than those that are located more remotely.

English, for instance, finds its closest linguistic relatives in the other Germanic languages of northwest Europe, like Dutch, Norwegian, and German - all of which developed in and are still spoken in countries relatively close by to England itself. Likewise, some of the French language's closest relatives include those spoken in neighboring Spain and Italy.

But in the world of linguistics, it's not uncommon to find an odd one out. That is a language that seems unrelated to or shares relatively little in common with those around it. Hungarian, for instance, has more in common with Finnish and Estonian than it does with the languages of Hungary's geographical neighbors. The Basque language of northern Spain is so unusual and unusual that linguists think it might have developed in total isolation and has no other relatives in the world today. And perhaps most bizarrely at all, Malagasy - the official language of the island of Madagascar, off the east coast of Africa - finds most of its closest relatives not just on the other side of the Indian Ocean, but in an entirely different ocean altogether!

Linguists have now discovered that despite Madagascar's geographical location, its native Malagasy language belongs to a family of around two dozen languages known as the Barito languages. These are spoken in a central region of

Borneo, in Indonesia. The Barito group is in turn thought to belong to an even larger group of languages known as the Malayo-Polynesian family. Most of these lie scattered across the islands of southeast Asia and the Pacific Ocean.

As a result, just as English is related to Dutch and French is related to Spanish, Malagasy's closest linguistic relatives include the likes of Hawaiian, Indonesian, Philippine Tagalog, Fijian, Malay, Tongan, and even Māori. All of those are spoken more than 5,000 miles away.

So how on earth has Malagasy come to be such an extreme linguistic outlier, isolated in its own world on the opposite side of the Indian Ocean?

It is thought that the Malagasy language developed sometime in the first millennium CE, initially among migrant boatmen who arrived in Madagascar from their homeland on the southeast Indonesian island of Java. Given the kinds of boats and navigational technology available, it was long presumed that these Austronesian settlers effectively island-hopped or 'port-hopped' their way there. They would have done this by gradually moving up and along the northern coast of the Indian Ocean, via the likes of Thailand, Myanmar, and India, before working their way down the Arabian Peninsula and the Horn of Africa to arrive at Madagascar.

In fact, chronological and anthropological evidence is now increasingly suggesting that these early Javanese arrivals may actually have taken a much more direct route. They may have gone due west from their home in Java and bravely headed out straight across the Indian Ocean in the hopes of finding land on the other side. This more drastic route is backed up by evidence from the Maldives islands, in the central Indian Ocean, where the remains of Javanese-style boats have recently been discovered. These suggest the ancient island hoppers used the Maldives archipelago as a midway stop-off point.

No matter the route they took to get there, it was these early Javanese migrants who brought their Austronesian language with them across the Indian Ocean to Madagascar, more than 1,000 years ago. There, it developed in relative isolation, disconnected from its closest linguistic siblings and ancestors by more than 5,000 miles. And so, it became one of the world's most extraordinary odd ones out.

Short And Sweet

In 1943, Hollywood legend Greer Garson was awarded the Academy Award for Best Actress for her powerhouse performance in the previous year's *Mrs Miniver*. Walking up to the lectern to give her acceptance speech, Garson was about to make history. Her speech, at a somewhat longwinded five minutes and thirty seconds in length, remains the longest speech in Oscar history.

Sadly, exactly what Garson said and who she found the time to thank in her winning address isn't entirely clear. The speech in full was not recorded, and even the archive of the Academy of Motion Picture Arts and Sciences has preserved less than four minutes of it. She never won an Oscar again, either (despite being nominated for a total of seven in her career) and so did not have the opportunity to change or redo her contribution to cinema history. Nevertheless, her record still stands to this day - not least because Oscar acceptance speeches have long since been limited to a very concise 45 seconds.

At the other end of the scale, however, is the Hollywood icon Patty Duke.

Two decades after Greer Garson, Duke took home the 1963 Academy Award for Best Supporting Actress for her role in *The Miracle Worker*, opposite that year's Best Actress winner, Anne Bancroft. Incredibly, Duke was just 16 years old at the time, and she remains one of the youngest-ever Oscar winners of all time. Only Anna Paquin (who was 11 when she won for *The Piano*) and Tatum O'Neal (who was ten when she won for *Paper Moon*) have been younger.

Perhaps due to her age, Duke was somewhat starstruck by the glitzy occasion. When she walked over to the lectern to give her acceptance speech, she simply said, "Thank you," and left the stage. It remains the shortest actor's acceptance speech in Oscar history.

Did You Know?

Seven More Famously Short Speeches

○ **THE 2ND INAUGURATION OF GEORGE WASHINGTON, 1793**

America's first president, George Washington, was inaugurated for the second of his two four-year terms in the Senate Chamber of Congress Hall in Philadelphia, Pennsylvania (at that time the nation's capital) on March 4, 1793. Opening with the words, "Fellow citizens," before famously going on to say that "I am again called upon by the voice of my country to execute the functions of its Chief Magistrate," Washington's second inaugural address lasted a mere matter of minutes. In total, he said just 135 words. It remains the shortest inaugural address in American history.

○ **JOE PESCI'S OSCAR ACCEPTANCE SPEECH, 1991**

Patty Duke isn't the only actor to have kept things brief at the Oscars. At the 63rd Academy Awards in 1991, Joe Pesci was awarded the Oscar for Best Supporting Actor for his role as New York crime baron Tommy DeVito in Martin Scorsese's *Goodfellas*. In doing so, he saw off stiff competition from the likes of Andy Garcia (as Vincent Corleone in *The Godfather Part III*) and Al Pacino (for his performance as Alphonse "Big Boy" Caprice, in the smash hit *Dick Tracy*). Walking up to the microphone to accept the award, Pesci's entire speech comprised just five words: "It's my privilege, thank you."

○ ALFRED HITCHCOCK'S OSCAR ACCEPTANCE SPEECH, 1968

Despite having one of the most illustrious movie-directing careers in Hollywood history, incredibly Alfred Hitchcock was nominated for just five Oscars, for the movies *Rebecca* (1940), *Lifeboat* (1941), *Spellbound* (1945), *Rear Window* (1954), and *Psycho* (1960). In each instance, the nomination was for Best Director. Even more incredibly, Hitchcock never won (and twice lost out to Billy Wilder, in 1945 and 1960). The Academy rectified the oversight in 1968 when Hitchcock was finally awarded the honorary Irving G Thalberg Memorial Award, which recognizes a life's work of consistently high-standard cinema. Having waited almost three decades for his moment on the Oscar stage, you might think Hitchcock would have made the most of the occasion. Instead, he spoke just five words and said simply, "Thank you. Very much indeed."

❍ WINSTON CHURCHILL'S ADDRESS TO HARROW SCHOOL, 1941

Two years into the Second World War, British Prime Minister Winston Churchill was invited to address the young students at his *alma mater*, Harrow School in London. The speech he delivered has since gone on to be considered one of his greatest. Against a backdrop of one of the darkest years in modern British history, Churchill gave a rousing address in which he memorably gave the simple lesson to "Never give in, never give in; never, never, never; never-in nothing, great or small, large or petty. Never give in." These simple words have since become the best-remembered line from Churchill's Harrow address - but the entire speech is by no means a long one. In total, Churchill used the opportunity to speak for only a matter of minutes and said just over 700 words in all.

❍ THE GETTYSBURG ADDRESS, 1863

Perhaps the most famous speech in American history is Abraham Lincoln's Gettysburg Address, with its famous opening line, "Four score and seven years ago." It was delivered on the afternoon of November 19, 1863, at the dedication of the Soldiers' National Cemetery (now the Gettysburg National Cemetery) in Pennsylvania, just over four months after the Battle of Gettysburg, the Civil War's bloodiest battle. Incredibly, Lincoln's speech was a somewhat impromptu affair and was not included in the event's official schedule. As a result, he kept his words brief. Despite its renown, the Gettysburg Address consists of just 271 words, and Lincoln spoke for barely three minutes.

○ LOU GEHRIG'S FAREWELL ADDRESS, 1939

Speaking to a packed Yankee Stadium on July 4, 1939, baseball star Lou Gehrig famously labeled himself "the luckiest man on the face of the Earth" in a farewell address that lasted barely two minutes. In all, one of the greatest players of all time said goodbye to the game with only 277 words.

○ ERNEST HEMINGWAY'S NOBEL LAUREATESHIP ADDRESS, 1954

Having narrowly survived two plane crashes, when Ernest Hemingway was awarded the 1954 Nobel Prize for Literature, he steadfastly refused to travel to Stockholm to accept the prize. Instead, he requested the United States Ambassador to Sweden, John M Cabot, read a speech on his behalf. Knowing that someone else was to read his words, Hemingway kept his acceptance speech brief. In all, he wrote just 334 words, ending with the memorable line, "I have spoken too long for a writer. A writer should write what he has to say, and not speak it. Again, I thank you."

A Lasting Impression

The list of achievements next to the Polish-French physicist Marie Curie's name in the scientific history books is truly remarkable. In 1903, she became the first woman in history ever to win a Nobel Prize, being awarded the prize for physics, alongside her husband Pierre Curie, for their work on radiation. In 1911, she became the first person - and the only woman in history - to win a Nobel Prize twice. That time, she was awarded the chemistry prize solo for her discovery of two new elements, radium and polonium (the latter named in honor of her native Poland). She and her husband - who won five prizes in total - remain the only married couple ever to have won a Nobel Prize. To this day, Marie Curie remains the only person in history to have won her pair of Nobel honors in two distinct scientific fields.

There is, however, an unfortunate aspect to the Curies' remarkable scientific endeavors. Although their contribution to our understanding of radiation and radioactivity is all but unparalleled, working more than a century ago, they were blissfully unaware of just how potent the radioactive forces with which they were working truly were. They could scarcely have anticipated their long-term effects.

At the turn of the last century, radiation was widely seen as little more than a scientific curiosity - as mysterious a phenomenon as it was wholly misunderstood. The bizarre energy that radioactive minerals and substances appeared to give off was for a long time wrongly considered to be a kind of medicinal tonic. Created draughts and even poultices and bandages containing radioactive material were often prescribed to patients suffering all manner of energy-sapping conditions.

This short-sightedness was mirrored by many of the early scientists who worked with radiation and radioactivity. In the late 1800s, the doctors and physicians who promoted the use of x-ray photography in medicine routinely exposed themselves to levels of radiation 1,500 times stronger than is considered safe today. As a result, many of them suffered from burns, hair loss, and skin blistering - and many more eventually succumbed to fatal conditions now linked to radiation poisoning.

Unfortunately, the Curies too were unaware of the consequences of working, day in and day out, with radioactive material. Both Marie and Pierre frequently fell ill from radiation sickness. It now seems likely that Marie's death at the age of 66 - attributed to a form of aplastic anemia - was likely caused by her work with radioactivity.

Not only that, but almost everything the Curies worked with remains radioactive to this day - from their clothing and the furniture in their laboratory, to their stationery and notebooks. These are kept in a lead-lined box in a specially sealed chamber in Paris, and can only be viewed by researchers by special request, and under strict health and safety guidelines.

These devastating aftereffects are not going to wear off any time soon, either. Incredibly, it has been estimated that the Curies' belongings - and even their bodies - will remain radioactive for more than 1,500 years.

A Dead Case

A few pages ago, we met Pope Gregory IX - the medieval Catholic leader who was so horrified by tales of cat-kissing devil-worshippers in Dark Age Germany, that he apparently turned much of Europe's opinion of cats on its head. Even with a feline holy war on his hands, however, Pope Gregory was by no means the strangest of the medieval world's papal leaders. This is illustrated by the bizarre story of Pope Stephen VI.

The events of this particularly strange episode in the history of Europe took place in the late 9th century. In 891 CE, the Vatican elected a new leader, Pope Formosus, who remained in power for the next five years until his death from a stroke (or, according to some more divisive reports, from poison). Although he remained steadfastly popular with the Catholic population, in those intervening years, Formosus proved a controversial figure within the church.

He stirred up opposition across Europe, setting the Vatican at odds with Constantinople, provoking the Muslim world, and throwing his weight behind schemes and campaigns only he personally supported. Case in point, at the time of his death in 896, Formosus was busy assisting in the raising of an army to support his favored claimant to the Holy Roman imperial throne, Arnulf of Carinthia.

After Formosus' sudden death, however, those plans ceased to be and the Vatican hastily installed his successor, Pope Boniface VI. Unfortunately, Boniface too died just 15 days in power (his reign was later declared null and void). This left a vacuum at the top of the Catholic church that an even more controversial figure, Pope Stephen VI, was only too quick to fill.

Stephen had been one of Formosus' staunchest opponents and had strongly disliked almost every element of his papacy. While Formosus had supported Arnulf, Stephen's preferred choice of Holy Roman leader was Arnulf's bitter rival, Lambert of Spoleto. With Stephen now in charge of the papacy, the Vatican suddenly changed its stance and allegiance, as Stephen put his full weight behind ensuring Lambert rose to the imperial throne. But that wasn't all he did to undo his predecessor's legacy.

In January 897, Stephen demanded that Formosus' body be exhumed. He ordered his corpse be hauled back to the Vatican chambers to be put on trial for charges of perjury and violating church canon law. This bizarre episode became known as the Cadaver Synod. As part of the trial, Formosus' body was dressed in papal finery and brought before Stephen, who angrily hurled questions and accusations at it.

Needless to say, Formosus couldn't exactly defend himself. So, Stephen promptly declared him to be guilty. He demanded Formosus be stripped of his robes, have his blessing fingers (the three middle fingers of his right hand) cut off, and his body tossed in a commoner's grave.

Perhaps predictably, Stephen's actions did not go down too well with Europe's Catholics. They still admired Formosus and did not believe the accusations thrown at him after his death. With unrest building across the Catholic world, the Vatican had Stephen ousted from power and imprisoned just a matter of weeks after his accession. He was strangled to death the following August. With that, one of the grisliest and most bizarre chapters in European history was finally brought to an end.

Yesterday Night

One night in December 1963, Paul McCartney awoke humming a simple melody that had underscored a dream he was having. Not wanting to forget it, he jumped out of bed and dashed across to his piano, where he began tapping out a relatively simple tune in F major.

McCartney was concerned that he had subconsciously recalled a song he had merely heard elsewhere. So, he spent the next several weeks asking anyone and everyone he knew in the music business whether they had heard the tune before. "Eventually it became like handing something into the police," he later recalled. "I thought if no one claimed it after a few weeks then I could have it."

In the end, nobody did recognize the tune, and it seemed as if the melody had indeed come to him while he was fast asleep and dreaming. Now, the next stage was to take this simple tune and turn it into a song. That meant coming up with lyrics to match it.

During a filming break for the Beatles' movie *Help!*, McCartney reportedly played the tune for John Lennon, who immediately saw its potential yet likewise struggled to come up with suitable words. (George Harrison seemed less immediately interested in it and reportedly commented that McCartney was "always talking about that song - you'd think he was bloody Beethoven or somebody!")

As they continued to work on it together, Lennon and McCartney began to use ludicrous placeholder lyrics in the absence of any serious words. They would sing to one another around the on-set piano, "Scrambled eggs / Oh my baby, how I love your legs / Not as much as I love scrambled eggs." Eventually, the situation proved too much for *Help!*'s director Richard Lester, who reportedly demanded that either McCartney finish writing the song, or he would have the piano removed. Happily, as John Lennon later recalled, all that McCartney needed was another good night's sleep.

"The song was around for months and months before we finally completed it," Lennon later explained. "Every time we got together to write songs for a recording session, this one would come up...We made up our minds that only a one-word title would suit - we just couldn't find the right one. Then one morning Paul woke up, and the song and the title were both there, completed."

The one-word title he had imagined? *Yesterday*.

Of Mice And Dogs

You've probably heard the one about the school kid who couldn't hand their homework in because their dog ate it. (Who knows, you may have once had cause to use that excuse yourself.) But as silly as it is, there is at least one famous instance of this unlikely explanation being absolutely true.

In the spring of 1936, the novelist John Steinbeck was busy working on the manuscript of his latest book. He was riding high on earlier successes like *Tortilla Flat* and his acclaimed 1932 short story anthology, *Pastures of Heaven*. Steinbeck's latest tale was shaping up to be an emotionally charged novella about two migrant workers in California, who travel from town to town seeking new employment opportunities at the height of the Great Depression. The book, he had decided, was to be titled *Of Mice and Men*.

Unfortunately, it wasn't mice Steinbeck had to worry about, but rather a dog - more specifically, his Irish setter puppy, Toby. As he later wrote in a letter to his editor, Elizabeth Otis, on May 27, a "minor tragedy" took place one night during the writing of *Of Mice and Men* when Toby, "left alone one night, made confetti of about half of my book." Around two months' work was unapologetically torn to shred. Given that Steinbeck preferred to handwrite his first drafts, there was no other copy in existence.

"I was pretty mad," Steinbeck went on, "but the poor little fellow may have been acting critically. I didn't want to ruin a good dog for a [manuscript] I'm not sure is good at all."

With two months' work now gone, Steinbeck suggested his deadline be set back around two months. At that point, he would send the final draft away for Otis to look at. Unaware that he was writing one of the greatest American novels of all time, he modestly ended his letter by saying, "I think [the book] has something, but can't tell much yet."

Did You Know?

Seven More Songs Written In Less Than An Hour

○ **SWEET CHILD O' MINE**

It may be one of the most famous openings in rock music history, but the introductory guitar riff of Guns N' Roses smash hit *Sweet Child o' Mine* was reportedly written by the band's guitarist Slash in a matter of minutes. The rest of the song was also largely pulled together there and then. The final epic production understandably took a lot longer to get right before the song was finally added to the band's 1987 debut album *Appetite for Destruction*, but most of it was set down in a half-hour jam session.

○ **WE ARE NEVER EVER GETTING BACK TOGETHER**

Taylor Swift reportedly wrote the lead single for her Grammy-winning album *Red* after a friend of Swift's then ex-boyfriend walked into the recording studio to ask whether rumors that she and he were reuniting were true or not. After the friend left, the record's producers, Max Martin and Shellback, asked Swift to elaborate on what had happened during the breakup and subsequent media frenzy. During the conversation, she picked up her guitar and began improvising the chorus to *We Are Never Ever Getting Back Together*. The rest of the song quickly followed, and the track was all but completed in just 25 minutes.

○ **(YOU GOTTA) FIGHT FOR YOUR RIGHT (TO PARTY)**
It may be one of the Beastie Boys' biggest hits, but they wrote the lyrics to *(You Gotta) Fight for Your Right (to Party)* in just five minutes, on napkins while backstage at the Hollywood Palladium in 1986.

○ **TOMORROW NEVER DIES**
When Sheryl Crow was approached to write the theme tune to the 1997 James Bond movie *Tomorrow Never Dies*, she reportedly knew almost instantly the sound and feel she wanted to use. Plus, given the film's enigmatic title, she already had a starting point for the lyrics. Incorporating the same style of the classic string-laden minor-key Bond themes written by the movie's long-time composer, John Barry, Crow later admitted that she and cowriter Mitchell Froom finished much of the song in around 15 minutes. Around 20 years later, Adele would go one better. It may have won her an Oscar, a Grammy, and a Golden Globe, but she wrote her Bond theme, *Skyfall*, in just ten minutes.

○ **SEVEN NATION ARMY**

White Stripes' frontman Jack White wrote the signature guitar riff of the band's 2003 smash hit *Seven Nation Army* in a matter of minutes. He did it while idly playing his guitar backstage during a soundcheck in Melbourne, Australia.

○ **(I CAN'T GET NO) SATISFACTION**

It's one of the Rolling Stones' biggest hits, but guitarist Keith Richards set down the track's iconic guitar part in just a few minutes. He did it using a tape recorder he kept by his bed and then promptly fell asleep. The song was finished the following day.

○ **SINGLE LADIES (PUT A RING ON IT)**

"When Bey came in," record producer The-Dream said of the day popstar Beyoncé recorded her anthemic smash hit Single Ladies, "she had that smirk that I see when I know a record is happening." Having explained the song to him, Beyoncé reportedly walked up to the microphone and recorded her vocals almost immediately; the song was all but completed in just 20 minutes.

Conclusion

And with that, our final INTERESTING STORY is done!

From wrestling kings to tragic queens, from moon-dwelling birds to gigantic treehouses, and from doomed expeditions to made-up towns, luckless scientists, brain-eating fungi, and radioactive notebooks, we've covered quite a few bases here. So, after all of this, what precisely have we learned?

Well, with the story of the coelacanth, we've bizarrely discovered that death is by no means the end—and so long as a creature remains hidden enough, there is always the possibility that it can come back from the dead!

We also found out that the reason the Oscar results are kept inside sealed envelopes - and only announced live on air - is because a newspaper broke the Academy's embargo more than 60 years ago!

And we've also discovered that if you mix the sound of a mating tortoise with that of a hissing goose and a squealing dolphin in heat, you apparently end up with something like a velociraptor...

Some of these stories are bizarre, and some of them are unbelievable. But it is probably fair to say that all of them have been interesting!

Made in United States
North Haven, CT
17 December 2023

45995287R00117